Reckless Love
Jesus' Call to Love Our Neighbor

Reckless Love
978-1-5018-7986-9
978-1-5018-7987-6 eBook

Reckless Love DVD
978-1-5018-7990-6

Reckless Love Leader Guide
978-1-5018-7988-3
978-1-5018-7989-0 eBook

Also by Tom Berlin

6 Decisions That Will Change Your Life

6 Things We Should Know About God

6 Ways We Encounter God

Bearing Fruit

Defying Gravity

The Generous Church

High Yield

Overflow

Restored

TOM BERLIN

RECKLESS LOVE

JESUS' CALL TO LOVE OUR NEIGHBOR

Abingdon Press / Nashville

RECKLESS LOVE
Jesus' Call to Love Our Neighbor

Copyright © 2019 Abingdon Press
All rights reserved.

Library of Congress Cataloging-in-Publication data has been requested.

978-1-5018-7986-9

Unless noted otherwise, Scripture quotations are from New Revised Standard Version Bible, copyright © 1989 National Council of the Churches of Christ in the United States of America. Used by permission. All rights reserved worldwide. http://nrsvbibles.org/

Scripture quotations marked (NIV) are taken from the Holy Bible, New International Version®, NIV®. Copyright © 1973, 1978, 1984, 2011 by Biblica, Inc.™ Used by permission of Zondervan. All rights reserved worldwide. www.zondervan.com The "NIV" and "New International Version" are trademarks registered in the United States Patent and Trademark Office by Biblica, Inc.™

19 20 21 22 23 24 25 26 27 28 — 10 9 8 7 6 5 4 3 2 1
MANUFACTURED IN THE UNITED STATES OF AMERICA

To Jim and Doug

After all these years, I am still looking up to and learning from my big brothers. I see in your lives so much of the good that Christ calls us to live out.

CONTENTS

CONTENTS

FOREWORD

One of the mistakes I have made in my desire to understand the teachings of Christ is to pay so much attention to his words that I barely notice his itinerary. This probably arises from the hundreds of hours I spent sitting in classrooms, lecture halls, and on pews listening to teachers, speakers, and pastors. My learning environments have almost always been sedentary, the kind of places that make you wish you had a good cushion. As one teacher told me, "The mind can only take in what the bottom can absorb."

Recently it struck me, while reading one of the Gospels, that Jesus is rarely still. He is a teacher with no classroom, an instructor who never told anyone to sit at a desk. Jesus is always in motion, moving from place to place. He is walking down roads, going into villages and cities, and along the way, he talks, teaches, and heals. Along the way, he picks up new disciples. None of them has a #2 pencil or notebook. The number one thing you seem to need when you become Jesus' disciple is a good pair of sandals. They are constantly on the move. Jesus sets both the destinations and the pace. Jesus never turns to his followers to say, "Where do you all want to go next?" Life with him was a long expedition to places you had never been, meeting people you often didn't hope to experience. His disciples are either right behind him or walking toward the destination he has told them to go to.

Jesus understood experiential learning. In three years, his followers met all sorts of people they would have never known without his direction. In many ways, Jesus was reckless.

- Rather than meet faithful Jews in the synagogue or Temple, Jesus' path took them to outcasts, Gentiles, Roman soldiers, women, people who were physically and mentally ill, and some said to be demon possessed.
- His followers watched Jesus debate with his detractors.
- They saw him rejected by old neighbors in his hometown.
- They saw him deal with the rich and powerful and comfort the poor and vulnerable.
- Rather than ridicule sinners, he forgave sins.
- While others gave those with leprosy a wide berth, Jesus walked right into their villages.
- When he heard of a man who lived among the tombs who was a danger to himself and others, Jesus got in a boat and went to look for him.

Jesus dove headfirst into situations that other people assiduously avoided.

You can't fully understand what Jesus teaches his disciples until you consider where he teaches it and what is going on when he speaks the words. There is a reason Jesus takes his disciples on this journey. There is a purpose to all of the activity. He wants to teach his disciples how to love God with all their heart, soul, mind, and strength. To do so, he has to teach them to love their neighbor as themselves.

I used to think it was just the opposite. I thought that one day I would learn to love God so plentifully that I would love my neighbor with the overflow. Loving our neighbor can be difficult in a number of ways. We can find it difficult to love our family, much less relate to people who are different from us. We want to play it safe. Love offered in our relationships is often calculated on a risk-to-reward ratio. Sometimes we want people to earn the love we offer. We give what we feel they deserve. We share what we believe they merit. Sometimes we dispense the ingredients of love, things like compassion, forgiveness, kindness, or forbearance, with the precision of a chemist mixing volatile compounds.

This human tendency to play it safe with our love may be the reason that Jesus was so reckless with his. *Reckless* is not a very positive word. You get a ticket for reckless driving. A reckless heart can lead to a tattered string of relationships that bring much drama and little satisfaction. A reckless disregard for the truth can land you in court. You can waste a fortune in reckless living.

Reckless love is different. It pushes us to cross all sorts of boundaries to help us love as God loves and commands us to love. Getting people to take a risk and do the unexpected is the kind of thing Jesus had in mind as he guided his followers to encounter surprising places and people. He has probably done something similar in your life if you have followed him for even a short length of time. Whenever we walk with Jesus, we have experiences that transform us. He takes us out of our comfort zones. Without apology or warning, he expands us, makes us afraid of what might happen, and then shows us how love is properly done. He is not content with sedentary faith.

As many have said, Jesus loves us enough to accept us as we are but too much to leave us as we are. This reckless journey from who we were to who we can become is what I want to consider with you in the pages ahead.

In order to live out the Great Commandment, to love God and love our neighbor, we have to learn to "be love" to those around us. The titles of the chapters of this book create an acronym that I hope will help you live out the commandment as you read. My goal was to create practical steps that readers could take on their journey of faithfulness to this way of life. These are the lessons I see in the journey Jesus made with his disciples. They are the lessons not just of the words he spoke, but the places they traveled, and the people Jesus introduced them to along the way. These are some of the processes that Jesus uses to help us take risks and be reckless in the love we show God, others, and even ourselves.

Begin with Love

Expand the Circle

Lavish Love

Openhearted Love

Value the Vulnerable

Emulate Christ

CHAPTER 1
BEGIN WITH LOVE

Do not waste time bothering whether you "love" your neighbor; act as if you did. As soon as we do this we find one of the great secrets. When you are behaving as if you loved someone, you will presently come to love him.[1]

C. S. Lewis

The most important thing is to know the most important thing.

I am about eight years old, a skinny wisp of a boy standing at the top of a high dive at the pool. I am so thin that it is possible that rather than dropping into the water, I might just float down, like a leaf in autumn. It is early in the morning. It was a slow climb up the ladder, and one that I only made because Coach Allen told me that this was the day that I would conquer the high dive. He said I would go off the high dive. He did not tell me how. Coach Allen gave swimming lessons, and they were more like a rite of passage than a way of learning to be safe in the water. Coach Allen did not offer suggestions. He gave orders. He called me "Berlin." It made me feel older, and more mature. It did not, however, make me feel more likely to conquer the high dive.

Coach Allen was short of stature but powerfully built. He was a retired Marine who exemplified why retired Marines are not called "retired." He did not have to talk about his time in the Corps for people to know it. When he greeted people on the street in our town, they would comment to each other, as he walked past, "You know, he was a Marine." And this was news to no one. He still had the haircut, the posture and the steely gaze of a man who has led other men. Coach Allen maintained a rigorous workout schedule throughout his life. He was lean. He was fit. He was a rock. And he was teaching me how to swim.

I look down and estimate the distance between me and the tiny body of water below. I am fairly certain it is about a mile and a half drop. I went to the pool years later as an adult. It was about eight feet, but I was taller by then, so it is all relative. Coach Allen knows I am hesitant. He tries encouragement, but I sense this is not a deep reservoir in his personality. "You can do this, Berlin. It's not as far as it looks. Go ahead now, get in the water."

I try to reason with him. I suggest that the next day would be better for me. I tell him that it might help if I thought about it first, maybe plan my entry into the water a bit, and practice by jumping off the low dive or even the side of the pool. I did not say that I was afraid, as I sensed that Coach Allen would have no understanding of that emotion. I said that the wind seemed to be picking up. It could throw me off. Seconds turn into a minute. One minute turns into five. I am stuck. I can feel impatience creeping into Coach Allen's voice.

Finally, I ask, "Why do I need to do this, anyway?" He said something I still remember today: "Because today is going to be a lot more pleasant for you if you go off the front of that diving board than if you come down that ladder to where I am standing."

I feel no concern for my safety with Coach Allen. I do not feel threatened, but I know there would be extra laps to inspire greater self-discipline for the boy who came down the ladder. The real motivation was that I did not want to disappoint him. I wanted to be more like him and less like the me I was being as I paced back and forth on the high dive. The drive to resolve this dilemma helps me understand the right question to ask in that moment: "Is there anything I need to know when I do this?"

Coach Allen fires back, "Just one thing: Jump!"

The most important thing was not the form. It was not how to position my arms or legs. It was not about the impact of hitting the water. The most important thing in that moment was to simply jump.

So, I jump.

When you know the most important thing to do, you are far more likely to do it.

THE MOST IMPORTANT COMMANDMENT

One day a teacher of the law came to Jesus. He wanted to know which commandment Jesus thought was the most important. You can see why. If you read the Hebrew Bible, you know there are a lot of commandments. Some say that there are 613 commandments. Some of these commandments are positively stated. They tell you what to do, like "honor your mother and father." Others are in the negative form. They tell you the things you should avoid, like "do not lie," "do not lust," or "do not run with scissors or you will poke your eye out." That last one is not in the Bible, but it is still good advice. Anyway, if you are trying to be obedient to God using the Hebrew Bible, there is a lot to remember when you are going about your day.

This particular teacher of the law knows the law. Beyond the law of Moses found in the Torah, the first five books of Hebrew Scriptures, this teacher of the law knows a lot of other rules that were developed when people asked how to specifically live out what was found in the Bible. He carries a unique burden, because people come to him for answers. Maybe he feels lost in the minutiae or maybe he has lost his way. He asks Jesus to distill it all down to the most important thing. The crowd grows quiet. Jesus says,

> The first is, "Hear, O Israel: the Lord our God, the Lord is one; you shall love the Lord your God with all your heart, and with all your soul, and with all your mind, and with all your strength."
>
> Mark 12:29-30

Jesus' followers smile because they know he nailed it. He quoted what Jewish people call the Shema. This text is first found in Deuteronomy 6:4-6. It was the first part of a prayer that they said in private and shared in worship in the synagogue. It was more than a prayer; it was a confession of their faith. The word *listen* or *hear* is the Hebrew word *shema*. Everyone agreed that it was the greatest commandment.

Many years ago, I heard a rabbi say that the great contribution of Judaism was not monotheism, the belief in one god. It was ethical monotheism, the understanding that the God you are worshiping is a God who is better than you, a God so good that you could not create this God in your purest and best moment. That is different from the religion of the Roman Empire that controlled Israel in the first century. They had many gods, all with distinct personalities. Jupiter was a control freak, which was understandable given that he was almost eaten by his father, Saturn, until his mother rescued him. His wife, Hera, was so jealous she turned women into monsters and once threw her own daughter off a mountain. Eros had a love addiction. Neptune was ill-tempered and unpredictable. Diana was distant and aloof and feared relationships, preferring to hunt animals alone.

What you may notice about these gods and goddesses is that they sound a lot like characters on reality TV shows today. They have human emotions and human issues. They are a volatile, dysfunctional lot. If you bought a house in their neighborhood you would look for a way out after the first block party. The pantheon of Roman gods was large and complicated. Those who ascribed to this religion had to offer sacrifices to different gods to get different things, from good crops to children who would get good grades and not talk back to their parents. If you read the stories of these gods closely, you realize that they are nothing more than reflections of their human authors. These gods act like us, but with superpowers and extreme mood swings, which is a very bad combination.

THE BEAUTIFUL GOD

When Jews said, "Hear, O Israel: The LORD is our God, the LORD alone" (Deuteronomy 6:4), it wasn't just an affirmation that there is only one God. It was a blessed relief. This one God, they believed, created everything and everyone. This was not some feuding clan of divinities like those of the Canaanites, Persians, Greeks, or Romans. The God of Israel was the one God with the genius to put stars in the heavens and give the earth an atmosphere that supported plants, trees, fish, and birds. This was the God of the land and the God who created the oceans.

When this God created humanity, it was for the purpose of living in a relationship of love with the created men and women, not abusing them or taking them as consorts. The God of Israel endowed human beings with intellect and strength and then gave them the responsibility to care for the creation in which they lived. It was a partnership. And when you went your own way and demonstrated that you were irresponsible and sometimes downright mean and selfish, God gave commandments that called you to be a better person than you would have ever been on your own. Pretty soon you told the truth, minded your manners and own business, respected your neighbor's life and property, and treated your mother and father properly.

When you did life God's way, you became trustworthy and kind. People wondered what had happened to you and how you changed, because they knew you before you knew God, and this is not what you were like. Back then, you were like everyone else. Sometimes you were a real jerk. But now you had a whole different way of life. You understood that the way of life God gave you was a real gift.

Israel loved the Lord because God was, in a word, *lovely*. They could see the beauty of God all around them in the faces of their children and every created thing, from the forest to the sunset to the spider in her web on the tree branch. They could see the same beauty in the way this good God was asking them to live, even as they struggled with the competing effect of impulses and desires that led them to think only of themselves and serve their worst inclinations. This is why the Shema proved essential to Israel and to its people in every generation. It was the touchstone, the standard or principle by which their lives would be judged.

When people varied from their love of God, they made other things the priority, whether it was their own desires or the temptation to make other commitments more important than their commitment to God. This is why sin is so often seen in the Hebrew Bible as a form of idolatry. To make something more important than God, to love something or someone more than the one God, was to worship something that did not merit this level of attention or dedication. This commandment to love God fully and completely was so important to the formation of every generation of the people of Israel that in the Book of Deuteronomy, they were told to teach it to their children as soon as possible. They were to wear the commandment on their person, and place it on the doorway of their home so that they would be reminded of it whenever they went into the world or returned to their family (Deuteronomy 6:1-25).

This love for God was not just a feeling they sometimes carried or a sensation they experienced during a religious practice like worship. Love of God was to be their primary commitment in life. It was to be the organizing principle of their decisions and day. To love God with all your being was to live God's way. This was the reason for the law and commandments. When a woman lived them out, she demonstrated that God was her true love. When a man was obedient, he showed that the life God described was the life to which he was most committed. Only through this unqualified love could the one God became the unifying agent of the life of the individual, family, and nation.

This is why Jesus so often talked about the importance of the condition of one's heart. To love God fully, you have to consider two important questions:

What bad things need to be cast out?

What good things need to be brought in?

LOVE YOUR NEIGHBOR

Nothing assists this assessment more than the second part of what Jesus said: "The second is this, 'You shall love your neighbor as yourself.' There is no other commandment greater than these" (Mark 12:31).

While the books of the Bible Jesus' followers would have heard read in the synagogue certainly spoke to the importance of loving one's neighbor in a variety of ways, Jesus was doing something a bit different here. This second commandment was not originally yoked to the Great Commandment. It is found in a list of assorted commandments in Leviticus 19: "You shall not take vengeance or bear a grudge against any of your people, but you shall love your neighbor as yourself: I am the LORD" (Leviticus 19:18).

Jesus offers us something quite powerful. He has taken all the lessons from God and put them into one essential summary statement that becomes the priority for the lives of his followers.

He also creates a real problem.

It sounds like a good idea to love your neighbor. In fact, it sounds virtuous and beautiful. But if you would have been in the crowd standing around Jesus that day listening to him debate the religious leaders, and if you would have turned your head and started examining exactly who your neighbor was, I bet you would have thought, "This is going to get tricky." There is the guy who lives next door to you who likes to stay up late, sit outside, and play the lyre into all hours of the night. To your left is the woman down the street, who always tells you, "I'm so worried about your children. I pray for them. They never seem well supervised. They could get hurt, or get into trouble. Especially the youngest one, he looks like trouble!" Across the way is the man who sells you fish in the market. His weights seem to be balanced in his favor. You pay the same amount every time but seem to come home with less and less. There are lots of nice people in the crowd as well, but you have discovered occasional moments where each of them is far from easy to love.

I have thought about the complexity of keeping these two commands for many years. There is a great deal of love in the world. It is important to remember this as we think about the power of these two commandments. Because Jesus put these two actions together, loving God and loving others, it is assumed in cultures deeply influenced by Christianity that expressions of love in the form of basic courtesy, kindness, respect, and thoughtfulness are the norm. It is when people experience a lack of these qualities that they cry foul. We know the people we want to be, and often are. At the same time, people often struggle to love even those closest to them. Families have conflict. Spouses can engage in hot arguments or cold neglect. Schedules can become so busy that there is not time to be thoughtful or even attentive toward those around you. We can hold grudges against others that expand like a fast-growing vine. What once was a small sprout of frustration after an unfortunate incident soon covers the relationship in a green canopy of resentment. Loving others is a tall order.

It is easy to think that if we learn to love God deeply enough, then loving our neighbor will be accomplished through the overflow of that relationship. There is much truth in this idea. Few things can help us love our neighbor like the transformation that is found when we learn to love God by accepting the forgiveness of Jesus Christ for our sins and following him as a disciple. When we learn from Christ and take the further step of becoming obedient to him as our Lord, it fills our lives with qualities and desires for good that may have been fully absent before we loved him. Paul lists these qualities and experiences when he says in his letter to the Galatians, "The fruit of the Spirit is love, joy, peace, patience, kindness, generosity, faithfulness, gentleness, and self-control" (Galatians 5:22-23).

However, there is another truth. It is only when we commit to love our neighbor and intentionally accomplish this goal that we learn what it means to fully love God. The reason is that nothing reveals what keeps us from fully loving God and growing in the likeness of Christ like attempting to love our neighbor. When I love my neighbor, I experience the rewarding feeling that comes when I am kind to another, or when I surprise someone with a thoughtful act that they appreciate greatly and did not anticipate. When I love my neighbor, I build up existing relationships and begin new ones.

BARNACLES ON THE SOUL

Conversely, loving my neighbor is the fastest way to identify all the rough spots of my soul. Here is just some of what I sometimes find when I try to keep the second commandment: resentment, lack of concern or compassion, prejudice, jealousy, bitterness, and blame. These are the barnacles on my hull.

Boat and ship owners have a number of unwanted marine organisms that collect on the hulls of their crafts. When bacteria, algae, and barnacles pile up, it is called fouling, or biofouling. It happens in stages. First bacteria join together to create a biofilm on the hull of the ship. This creates the perfect conditions for slime to form. Larger organisms that like nothing better than a nice bed of slime soon follow, like sponges, mollusks, tubeworms, mussels, and barnacles, along with their hard-to-pronounce cousins. Sometimes this all happens in the orderly fashion I have described, but other times the larger organisms just show up and invite their friends to come along and see the world with them.

Something similar happens when we cruise through life and encounter people. Many we get along with, but some we don't. There are disappointments, relational wounds, and bad habits that begin to attach themselves to our once pristine personality. Paul tells us that rather than reaching out in love, we turn inward in selfishness. When we do, the environment is just right for all sorts of bad things to attach themselves to our being. Paul describes it this way:

> The works of the flesh are obvious: fornication, impurity, licentiousness, idolatry, sorcery, enmities, strife, jealousy, anger, quarrels, dissensions, factions, envy, drunkenness, carousing, and things like these.
>
> Galatians 5:19-21

People can experience sin-fouling of the soul. I doubt all of Paul's list describes your life, but you may recognize a few of these items that have taken up residence on your personality. Over time, even one or two of the actions and attitudes that Paul observed can slow us down. They can also impact the people around us. They change our relationships and can change us. Happy people can become depressed. Hopeful people become pessimistic or cynical. Gracious people can become unforgiving. In our best moments, we want to get rid of all that has adhered to our soul, but like barnacles, sin has a cement-like rigidity that resists our best efforts at removal.

Biofouling damages a ship in many ways. Wood and metal begin to deteriorate. Surfaces become rough, which attracts more organisms and creates drag when the vessel is underway. The drag only increases as more and more barnacles and mollusks pile on for an all-inclusive crustacean cruise. The accumulated arthropods slow the ship down further and further as they grow larger and become more concentrated. The larger the ship, the more this increases fuel consumption and makes the vessel harder to maneuver and more expensive to operate. This is not a small problem. Across the shipping industry, biofouling adds tens of billions of dollars in additional fuel costs and hundreds of millions of tons of carbon dioxide emissions each year. Research is being done into new, environmentally-safe coatings to prevent biofouling on ships, along with the best practices for the removal of its accumulation. This sometimes requires the ship to be put in dry dock where saws are used to cut the biofoul off the hull and abrasives are used to recondition it. If the ship is left in the water, high pressure devices are used by divers who blast the organisms off the hull. This takes both time and money, and keeps the ship from being put in operation.[2]

Wouldn't it be great if there was a treatment for sin-fouled lives? By yoking these two commandments together, love of God and love of neighbor, Jesus offers us a way to unencumber our souls and keep them free over time. The pattern of loving God and loving neighbor creates a virtuous cycle that has a powerful outcome in the life of a Christ-follower. As we truly dedicate ourselves to loving God, we gain the ability to see ourselves clearly. We can identify what is sticking to our soul that must be scraped or blasted off. The light of God's love enables us to see how the grudges, animosity, bigotry, or contempt that has become a part of our personality slows down our sanctification and damages people with whom we come in contact on our journey.

Spiritual practices like learning the Bible, prayer, acts of service, participation in worship, baptism, the Lord's Supper, silence, or other means of grace help us grow in our love of God. As we come into a relationship with God that directs our choices and shifts our motivation from our own desires to God's love that reigns over us, a change takes place. We will have far greater experiences of patience, kindness, and self-control. These are the exact things that you need to fulfill the commandment to love your neighbor as yourself. You will need God to do this, because your neighbor also has a sin-fouled soul and may not have been dry-docked and cleaned off for years. This means that they will not always be easy to love.

When we attempt to keep the commandment to love your neighbor as yourself, we must realize that one imperfect and sinful person is attempting to love another imperfect and sinful person. Without God's help, there is a very low likelihood of that ending well. Barbara Brown Taylor puts it bluntly when she writes, "The hardest spiritual work in the world is to love the neighbor as the self—to encounter another human being not as someone you can use, change, fix, help, save, enroll, convince or control, but simply as someone who can spring you from the prison of yourself, if you will allow it."[3]

CONCEPT OR REALITY?

Often, we like the concept of loving our neighbor far more than the actual experience of it.

Years ago, Karen and I moved into a rental house in a nice neighborhood that our children enjoyed. As the fall turned into the winter, we started to feel the impact of the colder temperatures in our house. The time had come to turn on the heat. I walked over to the air vent and put my hand over it. I waited for warm air to rise, but all I could feel was a rush of air that was cold. I bumped up the thermostat from 68 to 70 degrees, and hoped it would get warmer. I held my hand over the air vent and felt no change. I thought, "You are being impatient. Give it some time."

Thirty minutes later, I came back to find the air coming from the vent was still cold. That was the night we learned that the house did not have "heat," it had a heat pump. Days later a friend stopped over. He observed that it was a little brisk in our home. When he heard about our dilemma, he shook his head and said, "Our last house had one of those." I showed him the thermostat and said, "The only way I can get warm air to come out is to turn up the thermostat until that green light comes on."

He said, "Don't do that! That is auxiliary heat. Use that and you will never be able to afford retirement."

I said, "But I'm cold. Karen is cold. The kids are cold. And all this thing does is blow cold air."

He said, "You can't think of it as cold. Think of it as very warm when compared to the outside temperature."

I said, "But it's 45 degrees outside."

He said, "Aren't you glad you aren't out there?!"

I said, "I think it is only about 60 degrees in here and I notice you are still wearing your coat."

He said, "That is the secret of a vintage heat pump. Lots of layers."

The problem was that our heat pump didn't think of heat as a verb. It believed in heat as a concept, but that did not mean that it would heat our home in the sense of actually being warm. Lots of people explained to us the concept of the heat pump, how it took air across coils and made it warmer than the outside air. We nodded attentively and said, "Yes, but we are cold!"

They said, "You will be cold until the Spring. The heat pump works very well in the Spring."

Many of us love our neighbor the way that heat pump warmed our house. We think of love as a concept. We want to be a loving spouse or parent, a loving friend or neighbor, which sounds good and even easy. Jesus is calling us to love, not as a concept, but as a verb. To accomplish this is the work of a lifetime. It must be the centering principle of our days. Love must be infused in our conversations. Carry it as your outlook. It is hard to stand in a grocery store when you run into a coworker and gossip about your boss if love is your guide. Likewise, it is easy to wait patiently for the new check-out clerk who is trying to figure out the code to enter as she weighs your bananas when love is foundational to the way you interact with others.

At the same time, loving your neighbor will enable you to appreciate the beauty of God in new ways. As a result, you will find yourself more attracted to God and more in love with the one who created all these people you have grown to know and appreciate.

The link that Christ made by joining these two commandments was not linear, but circular. When we love both God and our neighbor, we enter a virtuous cycle that transforms our lives. Loving God enables me to love my neighbor, and loving my neighbor enables me to fully love God. Until I learn to love my neighbor, until I fully commit to that task, I will never fully love God. This is true not only because my neighbor carries a unique reflection of the image of God, but also because the act of loving another is the fundamental matter of God's character and being. The author of 1 John states this succinctly: "Beloved, let us love one another, because love is from God; everyone who loves is born of God and knows God. Whoever does not love does not know God, for God is love" (1 John 4:7-8).

It is important to understand why this is important to Jesus. Christ's goal is nothing less than full transformation of your life. His desire is for you and me to gain the same loving nature as our Creator. While loving God is a noble pursuit, it is not that difficult to love a benevolent and wise being who has created the universe you inhabit and crafted your life as well as everyone you value. It is quite another to love the couple next door whose dog routinely uses your flower bed as a toilet.

BEGIN WITH LOVE

Where do we begin to keep the Great Commandment? At the beginning. Here are three powerful words: *begin with love*.

Say these three words out loud or consider them in your mind and they will have great effect on your day. Open your eyes in the morning and think, *begin with love*, and you will be likely to start your day in prayer to the God who loves you and offer gratitude for your life, no matter your circumstances. When you have your first conversation of the day, think again, *begin with love*, and you will be far more likely to listen in a way that honors the other person and talk about what might interest them. Later in the day you will drive somewhere. Someone behind you will run right up to your bumper and may even flash their lights at you. Think to yourself, *begin with love*, and you will find yourself carefully changing lanes rather than considering what you want to say to that person or what gesture you want to use as your reply to their rude behavior. You will interact with people you don't know well, like the cashier at the store. *Begin with love* and you will be both pleasant and kind. You may have a conversation with a child who is demanding or a coworker who disagrees with you on some element of a shared project. As *begin with love* goes through your mind, you will find that it will alter the way they experience you. It may throw them off balance a bit as they expect you to become inflexible or stubborn.

Beginning with love prevents sin barnacles from taking up residence on our souls. One of the habits I have that can displace love is blame assignment and stating the obvious when something goes wrong. It goes this way: Karen comes home after work and a stop at the grocery store. Her hands are full of grocery bags. As she enters the house, the door is left open and the dog gets out. Rather than look for the dog, I pause and say, "You left the door wide open when you came in with those groceries. Now the dog ran off! I'll go look for him!"

Assigning blame and stating the obvious does not help you find a canine escapee. It does change the dynamics of our relationship. Long after the dog comes loping back up the driveway, the conversation is terse and in need of repair.

Contrast that to times when as a husband, I honored those three magic words, *begin with love*. The other day, Karen was recounting a story to someone that happened more than twenty years ago. I had forgotten the details. She remembered them all. I was away on a church mission trip to Africa. It snowed hard one night. By morning the accumulation was nearly a foot of snow. She needed to clear the driveway amidst caring for our three children. After setting up the rare treat of a snow day movie and snack, she hurried out the front door and shoveled the walk. She shoveled her way down the driveway, checking periodically on our young children, and then returned to shoveling until a path was cleared from the garage to the street. Satisfied, she went indoors to warm up before heading out for some needed groceries.

When she entered the garage and pressed the door opener, she realized she had a problem. She had shoveled the wrong side of the driveway! Her van was on the other side of the garage, which had two doors. The lane she cleared was for the other side. In order to get the van out of that side, she would have to shovel the other half of the driveway which would take hours more. It was then that it occurred to her that a more immediate solution would be to turn the minivan around inside the garage and drive it out of the other side. As amazing as it sounds, it all went quite well until she went to pull out. That is when the van ripped the garage door rail off the wall and twisted it in half.

As she recounted this story, I noticed that the story she was sharing was less about the details recounted above, and much more her amazement at my reaction when she showed me the damage she did to garage and van. Karen said that I looked at the twisted metal and said, "Well, that's something that we can get fixed. I'll look into it tomorrow." In that instance, it looks like I simply began with love. Karen had expected and anticipated many things, but that moment of love was so meaningful that she remembered it more than twenty years later as an act of grace in our relationship worthy of retelling.

How I wish I had given her a hundred memories like that one.

Such moments were the intention Jesus had when he took the Shema and yoked it to the second commandment, "You shall love your neighbor as yourself" (Mark 12:31). Love is not a principle in which we believe. It is not an aspiration we hope to attain. It is an orientation that sets the course of our daily words and actions. There are three places where it is vital:

- Conversations in which you partake. To *begin with love* will dramatically impact how you listen, what you say, and how you say it.
- Assumptions you make. When you *begin with love*, you will assume the best about others instead of the worst.
- Actions you undertake. The mind of a person who says *begin with love* is more thoughtful of others. In matters small and large, you will begin to bless people around you in ways that may surprise both you and them.

These three powerful words, when intentionally spoken, will set the course of words, assumptions, and actions of a person who works to honor the Great Commandment to love God and neighbor. We need to begin with love because when we begin to act on the Great Commandment, we discover that God is putting people in our lives that will challenge our ability to be consistent. When these people show up, and become a part of your circle of relationships, you will think that God is just messing with you, because you will find some of them really difficult. You may even believe that it is not possible to love them. The truth is, God is messing with you. The Lord is pushing you to activate the virtuous cycle. When you learn to love that particular hard-to-love neighbor, you will discover things about God, and learn to stand in wonder of God, in ways you would not have discovered without that neighbor.

CHAPTER 2
EXPAND THE CIRCLE

The older I get, the more I meet people, the more convinced I am that we must only work on ourselves, to grow in grace. The only thing we can do about people is to love them, to find things to love in them.[1]

Dorothy Day

Since I was a child, my favorite Christmas video has been *How the Grinch Stole Christmas!*[2] You know the story. The Grinch is a mean one. He hates Christmas. No one is sure of the reason, but Dr. Seuss tells us,

> It *could* be his head wasn't screwed on just right.
> It *could* be, perhaps, that his shoes were too tight.
> But I think that the most likely reason of all
> May have been that his heart was two sizes too small.[3]

Grinch makes his dog Max go with him to Whoville, where he steals all of the decorations, gifts, and food. He is sure he will ruin Christmas. To his astonishment, on Christmas morning all the Whos down in Whoville join in their Christmas chorus and celebrate anyway. It is at this moment that two things happen simultaneously: first, the Grinch understands the true meaning of Christmas—a joy that extends far beyond decorations, food, or gifts—and second, the sled that contains all of that stuff begins to slip over the side of the mountain.

> And what happened, *then*? Well in *Who*-ville they say
> that the Grinch's small heart grew three sizes that day.
> And then—the true meaning of Christmas came through,
> and the Grinch found the strength of ten Grinches,
>   plus two![4]

As the narrator shares that line, a little x-ray machine appears that allows us to see the Grinch's heart. My favorite moment is when the metal frame on the x-ray goes "poinggg!!" as the Grinch's expanding heart breaks through.

Then, and only then, does the Grinch have both the will and the capacity to rescue the sled and return its bounty to Whoville. No one is more surprised than the Grinch when he steps into the circle of Whos and sings along.

Christ's reckless love for us is like that. Its love-enlarging capacity disrupts some of the assumptions that define our living. Capacity is an important concept that influences human productivity, health, and well-being. Perhaps you know the person who wants to do it all, says yes to everything, but then experiences mediocrity or failure because of time commitments that exceed the defined hours in a day. There are businesses and organizations that flounder when their endeavors are stretched beyond their financial or personnel resources. Likewise, there are those that succeed and thrive precisely because of the careful consideration of capacity, made prior to their undertakings. I experience capacity issues, and suspect you do too. Life has taught us that our resources are finite and must be stewarded and managed selectively.

Jesus' example and ministry disrupt our ideas about the limited capacity of love. Mothers and fathers discover when they become parents of a second child that love is not divided, but exponentially multiplied. It is not restricted by conditions or number, but comes fully to each child. In the same way, we find that God's love is limitless.

When I was a child, we sometimes ate Sunday dinner at my Great-Aunt Ibbie's house. She carried this unusual name because when my father, as a boy, said "Elizabeth," it came out "Ibbie." Apparently, they thought it fit her better. It was a rare event to hear the family call her anything else. I loved my great-aunt and I loved her house. Both were warm, welcoming, and spacious. When my brothers and I entered that house, Ibbie would hug our necks and kiss our cheeks. She was a school teacher and she loved children. She knew all the right questions to ask and she often told adults to wait a minute while she finished hearing about our week or how school was going, which made you feel like you were a big shot even if you were only in second grade. She left you with the impression that she saw some secret quality in you that no one else had seen, which you would one day realize about yourself when you looked down on earth from your spaceship or won your Nobel Prize.

Aunt Ibbie could cook. Pot roast, macaroni and cheese, green beans in country ham, sweet potatoes, beets, and turkey and gravy. Sundays were considered holy days by our family in part due to the invitation to join together for a midday dinner at Ibbie's. The seating started in the dining room. Uncle Charles, the family patriarch, sat closest to the kitchen door. Uncle Carl sat on the far end of the room, so that he could leave early to watch the football game or blow smoke rings from his cigar that he could send right up your arm. He got away with such habits because he was family by marriage.

The younger generation found chairs at TV trays in the living room. On some occasions, the number of family present meant that people spilled out onto the porch. By the time my brother was sixteen, he was 6 feet, 2 inches tall, and was balancing a TV tray on his knees. As it hovered above the floor, he muttered that the system made no sense. Everyone at the table was shorter than him. We knew, however, that even if we grew to be 8 feet tall, we would not be seated at that table any time soon. It was a capacity issue. A seat at the table was not about height. It was about your place in the family. Defined by limited chairs and space, table seats were first reserved for my grandparents' generation, Ibbie's brothers and sisters and their spouses. Next came my parents' generation, by order of birth. There was only one way to move into a coveted spot at the dining room table, and it was not something you would ever hope for. The death of a loved one would bring a chain reaction to the seating assignments to fill the seat at the dining room table.

Capacity necessarily and effectively defined dinner seats at Ibbie's, but it had no reign on love. Regardless of your age, one thing you could be sure of at Ibbie's was that you were loved. Her house was a place where our family learned about God's reckless love, where capacity was not constrained by limited seats around the table, but expanded in the arms that enfolded you when you entered and joined the feast, no matter where you sat.

EXPAND LOVE OF YOURSELF

It is often not until Christ enters our lives that we recognize the expansive, capacity-free nature of God's love. One area where I have found it particularly hard for people to comprehend God's reckless love is the specific love God has for them. It is often easier for people to believe that God loves the world than believe that God loves just them. When we realize that we are loved by God, it becomes easy to love ourselves. Consider

Simon, a fisherman who lived in Capernaum, on the Lake of Gennesaret, also known as the Sea of Galilee. He had a reckless encounter with Christ and came away a changed man as a result.

Jesus asked Simon if he could use his boat. A large crowd had gathered on the shore and Jesus needed to set out into the water so that he could speak to them. When the teaching was over, Jesus told Simon to go out into the deep part of the lake and put down his nets. Simon rolled his eyes. (I do not know this from reading the Bible. I know it from being with people who know how to fish. Those with skills and experience do not like amateurs offering suggestions.) Simon told Jesus that they had been fishing all night with no success, but out of respect, did as the teacher suggested. He put out further from the shore and let down the net, confident that nothing would happen. Suddenly the net was so full of fish that Simon was yelling for help. Simon's fishing partners, James and John, came to assist. The haul was so great that it almost sank both boats.

Simon had fished this lake a long time. He knew what Jesus just did was a miracle. This set off a bit of a chain reaction in his brain. Simon saw a miracle and knew it was connected to someone holy. That made him think about all the aspects of his past and present life that were unholy. Luke writes, "When Simon Peter saw it, he fell down at Jesus' knees saying, 'Go away from me, Lord, for I am a sinful man!'" (Luke 5:8).

I wonder if Simon knelt down on the shore or in the boat full of fish? Either way, he knew something smelled bad beyond the tilapia. Simon, filled with self-awareness, knew that he was not worthy to be in Jesus' company. Simon had secrets that he assumed Jesus did not know. Knowledge about who we really are, or who others have told us we are, can be a barrier to loving ourselves.

If you want to expand your love for yourself, then you have to deal with what you see when you look inside yourself. Feelings and memories we bury and try to ignore are likely to come in two forms: shame and guilt.

I tend to connect shame to the things that others have done to you. For example, a woman who has been sexually assaulted may carry a secret shame. It is not shame for her actions. She told the man "no." She pushed him away. She was not asking for it. It wasn't how she dressed or something that she said. It was what the man did, this violation of her body and dignity that makes her shudder and choke when she thinks about it years later.

Shame includes the memories you carry from people who treated you as something less than a child of God. They acted as if you were an object to be made fun of or a transaction that was not bringing them sufficient return. Sometimes shame comes from words, unfounded statements and judgments yielded against you, or an act of bullying or deceit that you endured. No matter how it happens or how deep it tunnels inside your head, secrets of shame make us want to shrink our relationships. We isolate ourselves from others, so that we won't be hurt again or have others find out that we could not keep someone from hurting us in the first place. Shame deflects love. It tells us we are not worthy of love.

Another powerful kind of secret comes in the form of guilt. I tend to think of guilt as things we did all on our own that wounded ourselves or others. Relationships that were neglected. Something you stole. Gossip you shared about someone that was spread far and wide that later you learned was utterly untrue. Guilt is a whiteboard full of words that remind us of our sins that seem to have been written in permanent marker. No amount of effort we apply removes them from our memory. We sometimes can clearly recall the faces of the people we have hurt. Often one person's guilt leads to another person's shame.

Like Simon, we keep these parts of ourselves hidden because we want people to think well of us. We bury them because we want to be a part of a community and to have friends; and we fear that if people knew our secrets, that might be lost. The biggest problem with shame and guilt is that as long as we carry either, it is hard to love ourselves. Both obstruct the good things that others celebrate in us. Every time we look at our good qualities, shame and guilt photobomb us and ruin the picture. It is easier to be alone, in a self-imposed solitary confinement. That is probably why Simon tells Jesus to go away.

Jesus knows that we need him to help us deal with our shame and guilt. Shame does not need forgiveness, because it involves what others have done to us. We don't need to be forgiven for being hurt, but we do need to heal. Treating shame takes honesty rather than confession. We don't need to repent so much as we need to rediscover God's beauty within us. God's image is embossed on our souls. It is hard to see, under that grimy film others left behind, but shame can be cleansed. It has to be removed carefully, kindly, and often slowly. It takes time and patience and often the demonstrated love of close friends or wise counselors, but restoration is possible. Our hearts can grow this way and give us room for friendship and love to share with others.

Guilt needs forgiveness. We have to finally realize who got hurt as the result of our anger, the relationship we tainted or the person we degraded with our lust. We have to appreciate the impact of our lies. We must finally understand that our adultery tore apart a marriage or impacted somebody's kids. We need to see the trust we degrade or the livelihood we diminish by theft before we become repentant.

Often you and I have the same impulse as Simon. Just at the moment that we need Jesus to set us free from guilt, we are mortified to be in his presence. Jesus knows us, which is why he looks at Simon and says, "Do not be afraid; from now on you will be catching people" (Luke 5:10b).

Our fear is that God's love is not expansive enough to heal our wounds or gracious enough to forgive our sins. Our thinking can be so limited that we can't imagine that God is able to do what we have been unable to accomplish for ourselves. Jesus orders Simon to give up his fears. It is apparent from reading the Gospels that Jesus knows what is going on in the lives of everyone he meets, the same way he knows about all the stuff in your life and mine. Jesus called Simon to join him as he was. He did not make him confess his sins, get a higher SAT score, or improve his resumé for a few years and reapply. Jesus knew he could expand Simon's capacity to love by offering him grace. When we realize that God has a heart for us, it enables our hearts to expand. That experience may be what allowed Simon to put his shame or his guilt in perspective. It may be why Jesus later changed Simon's name to Peter, to focus his attention on his strengths and future rather than on his past.

Christ sees so much in each of us that we often do not see in ourselves. His love is complete. His forgiveness is unsurpassed. This is his special grace to us: Jesus will overcome our past and show us new possibilities, if we allow him. In opening yourself to the love Christ has for you, loving yourself gets a whole lot easier.

EXPAND YOUR LOVE OF OTHERS

You have to hand it to Simon. His response is as reckless as Jesus' offer. James and John were right behind him. "When they had brought their boats to shore, they left everything and followed him" (Luke 5:11).

Simon, James, and John walk away from their old lives to follow Jesus' call to reach people. Jesus is not transactional in his relationships. Jesus did not call them because they were going to be the best at sharing his message with others. He didn't want to see what he could do *with* their lives. Jesus wanted to show them what he could do *in* their lives. Jesus' love for us and the calling he offers to us is not about how many talents or resources that we bring, as helpful as they can be. Jesus' desire is to simply set us free to love others.

Jesus is assembling a group that will be together for nearly three years. They will travel by foot, walking together every day from place to place.

They will often sleep out in the open, between cities and towns Jesus wanted to visit. They will have to figure out where to find food, water, and fuel for fires. They will learn to depend on each other deeply. When they find shelter, they will be in close quarters. There will be little privacy, few comforts, and less showers. Essentially, it would be a three-year camping trip.

When Karen and I were first married, we went across the United States for two months. While we stayed with friends for a few nights, for the rest of that time we lived in a tent or slept in the back of our covered pick-up truck. We left with a case of tuna, a cooler full of food and full tank of gas. We spent almost every minute of every day together, driving, hiking, or enjoying time cooking and sitting by a fire at our campsite. We saw national parks and natural beauty that the years have not diminished. Conditions were not always perfect. Heat and rain could make the day long and sleep scarce.

One night we camped in Glacier National Park in a campsite where the ground was unusually hard. After bending a few stakes, I gave up trying to anchor our tent. The wind began to blow soon after we lay down that night. Our tent would expand with air and then flap about with every gust. It sounded like we had laid our sleeping bags in a wind tunnel. I doubt I slept more than an hour that night. When the sun rose, I decided to get into our truck, where I hoped to escape the constant noise. In only a few minutes I was starting to doze off when I heard an odd noise. Just audible over the wind in the sealed cab of our truck, I could hear something that sounded like someone was shouting. I opened my eyes and realized that our tent was no longer next to the truck. It was rolling across the open field. It took a few moments for it to register in my brain that Karen's slight frame was not sufficient to anchor the tent in such high winds. She was still inside. Every time she tried to open the tent, another gust would send it rolling several more feet. It was a few additional moments before I was able to catch the tent, collapse the poles whose form effectively made it a sail, and help Karen get out. By the end of that summer we realized that two months of camping would either lead to a deep and cherished relationship, or a homicide. I felt both honored Karen stuck with me and grateful to be alive. I can't imagine what three years of such living could do to a group of twelve guys following an itinerant rabbi.

It would seem like a good idea for Jesus to pick disciples who worked well in teams, were compatible, amicable, or helpful. Instead, Jesus' next choice is a tax collector for the Roman government. The Romans had conquered Israel and most of the known world. Rome used the power of its army to keep the peace and gain wealth by taxing those who lived there. You can imagine the resentment created when people were charged a toll to use a road that had once been free for everyone, or when other taxes were collected and sent to distant Rome to be used by a pagan emperor. No one liked Rome except the Italians. Tax collectors were one of the most hated groups because they took your money without giving you voice or vote for its use. They were authorized to then take on a bit extra as their personal commission. When people wondered out loud why any citizen of Israel would accept a job collecting taxes for Rome, the motivations offered ranged from "traitor" to "greedy."

Levi was a sinner. There was no hiding it. It was apparent every time he showed up for work. "Tax collectors and sinners" is a phrase that appears in the Gospels to denote a subgroup of people who were social outcasts and despised by the general population. It had to strike Simon, James, and John as odd when Jesus started to talk to Levi. We don't know what Jesus said, or what questions Levi may have asked him. We do know what happened as a result.

> After this he went out and saw a tax collector named Levi, sitting at the tax booth; and he said to him, "Follow me." And he got up, left everything, and followed him.
>
> Luke 5:27-28

For Jesus this is an opportunity for another transformed life. For Simon, James, and John, this is an endless camping trip with Levi, a blood-sucking parasite who is a minion of the Empire. It is in this calling of the fourth disciple that we discover a whole new meaning to the instruction to "love your neighbor as yourself."

Before Levi leaves town, he invites Jesus and his new friends to meet all of his old friends at a big dinner at his home. His tax collector buddies are all there, along with an assorted group of other people whose sins were well-known to those who lived in the villages and towns around Lake Gennesaret. These people did not receive too many invitations. People would have crossed the street to avoid them. They would not have been accepted at the synagogue. The local religious authorities were in the majority opinion when they complained to Peter, James, and John, "Why do you eat and drink with tax collectors and sinners?" (Luke 5:30).

Had Simon responded, I wonder if he would have said, "I have no idea. Truly. I have been wondering the same thing myself all day. When I joined up, I had no idea that guy was a part of the deal."

But Jesus was clear. "Those who are well have no need of a physician, but those who are sick; I have come to call not the righteous but sinners to repentance" (Luke 5:31-32). To be chosen and commissioned by Jesus was a great opportunity. You got a back-stage pass when Jesus taught the crowds. Later you could ask him questions and clarify what you did not understand. You could observe the rabbi up close. But critical to the teaching climate that Jesus created was the decision to expand the disciples by putting them with people who would stretch them.

Few of them were the kind of people you would expect a self-respecting itinerant rabbi to invite to join him. We have heard about Peter and Levi. Mark tells us that Jesus called James son of Zebedee and John the brother of James "Boanerges, that is, Sons of Thunder" (Mark 3:17). I have wondered if this described a temper problem, or possibly what happened when the brothers ate too many lentils.

Jesus' disciples included the good, the bad, and the ugly. There was Nathanael, of whom Jesus said, "Here is truly an Israelite in whom there is no deceit!" (John 1:47) and Andrew, who was once a follower of John the Baptist. Phillip was from the same hometown as Simon Peter. Little is known about Thaddeus. There was Thomas, who on the one hand proclaimed, "Let us also go, that we may die with [Jesus]" (John 11:16), only later to say, "Unless I see the mark of the nails in his hands, and put my finger in the mark of the nails and my hand in his side, I will not believe" (John 20:25).

There was Simon the Zealot, a man so devoted to Jewish law that he would have considered warfare with the Romans to be an honor and a duty. And of course, there was Judas Iscariot, the one who brought the soldiers to arrest Jesus. He was another financial guy, the treasurer of the group who sold out Jesus for thirty pieces of silver.

Jesus could have chosen twelve men with the same backgrounds, interests, outlooks, and perspectives on life. Instead, he does just the opposite. Jesus chooses followers who would not like or trust each other based on their reputations and former lives. All they really had in common was a willingness to leave everything and follow Jesus. When Jesus assembles this group, he is not simply calling together random strangers for a one-time selfie of the rabbi and the sinners. He is inviting each one to join him, to do life together, both with him and with each other.

How different this odd mix of people is from our society today, where increasingly people cluster into ideological echo-chambers where membership is earned by agreement on a few essential issues and the information people consume is often determined by what affirms their worldview. It is different from many churches that, in the name of adherence to the Bible, gather with like-minded Christians who then look down on other so-called Christ-followers when they read the same Scriptures but come to different conclusions. Church members in recent years are more prone to leave a congregation when the pastor preaches even one message that is considered by them to be coloring outside the lines on an important social issue. They may find fellow members of the congregation equally untenable based on social media posts or after hearing an opinion shared in a small group or over coffee before a service. Churches that once enjoyed a broad array of members who were bound by a common love of Christ are now sometimes defined by a narrower adherence to a select cluster of conclusions that are seen as the litmus tests of the true faith. The saints of glory have been substituted with the saints of uniformity.

One look at the group Jesus first assembled as his followers tells us that something is lost when sameness is the defining characteristic of a church. Jesus' example teaches us that something is wrong when we leave out people who differ from us and only feel at home when everyone is the same. His goal is not to make us more of what we are, but help us to become what we can be. That requires us to expand our understanding of what it means to love our neighbor. Christ shows us that the only way to learn the greatest commandment is to have people in our lives who we personally find so difficult to love that we have to get up every morning and pray to our Creator for a love we could not produce on our own. The first disciples had to ask God to expand their hearts so they could overlook the past sins of the tax collector, put up with the ideological torpedo the zealot launched at breakfast, ignore the angry brothers' latest argument, or figure out if it was time to confront the group treasurer they were beginning to think was embezzling funds.

Think for a moment about your own circles: neighbors, friends, members of the church you attend, or people you know from work. Undoubtedly there are some people you find harder to love, or some you may believe are impossible to love. What if Christ rejoices in our being with each other so that we can learn what it truly means to love our neighbor—every neighbor—as ourselves? What if it is the hope of the Holy Spirit to lead us to greater diversity rather than less? Jesus calls us to a different way of life when he says, "If you love those who love you, what credit is that to you? For even sinners love those who love them. If you do good to those who do good to you, what credit is that to you? For even sinners do the same" (Luke 6:32-33).

Christ's intentionality in selecting the twelve initial disciples may have been less about tolerance building and more about love expansion. Sophia had been a member at Floris United Methodist Church for some time before I became the pastor. I don't know how she even found the church because she never lived near it. I asked someone and he said, "I think God just sent her." Sophia was from Ghana. When she first attended Floris it was a small, mostly white, congregation. If Floris UMC was mashed potatoes, Sophia soon became the pepper. Red pepper. She was a spice that gave us a new and more vibrant flavor, and helped make us the more diverse church that we are today. She was a formidable presence. She was beautifully dressed for church every Sunday, just as she would have been in Ghana. Her regal nature demonstrated itself in other ways. She spoke her mind and sometimes acted on things before a group had any real agreement on a plan. Sophia was always ready for us to get on with the work of the church.

Sophia's middle name was Nana. I am not sure what that refers to in Ghana, but in the United States, "Nana" is what children often call their grandmother. Sophia was single and had no children of her own, so she loved everyone else's. She was a tireless volunteer at Hutchison Elementary, our partner school down the street. Sophia read books, played games, and had lunch with children for years so that they would know they were loved.

She taught Sunday school at the church and wanted to share her love of God and the lessons of Christ with new generations. Over the years she spent time each summer as a leader at vacation Bible school and at our summer school program at Hutchison. She helped children learn how to play in the bell choir.

The nice thing about Sophia was that she never forgot a child. She would bring you a giant plastic container of pretzels and tell you to take it to your daughter or son in college because she once taught them in Sunday school. She once brought me a box of dishes and silverware when she heard one of our daughters was moving from a dorm room to an apartment. When I suggested that she already had what she required, Sophia said self-assuredly, "She will need these. Take this to her."

It was not an offer. It was a command.

Each year our church rehabilitates a home with a local chapter of Rebuilding Together. Sophia was in charge of refreshments for that project for many years. Sophia would be given a budget, say $120, for food for the day. A few days after the event, she would walk in the church office with a stack of receipts that totaled over $200. When reminded of the $120 limit, she would simply say, "Well, it could not be properly done for that amount."

Sophia walked by faith as much as anyone I knew. Sometimes it confounded me. She made such assumptions. She would sign up to drive people to a doctor's appointment when her car was broken. When I asked her how she was going to do that, she would say that God would provide. She would call a friend or a taxi. It could be frustrating, but she lived by faith that God was in the details, that God could be trusted. She had lived alone for many years and combined her own habits with confidence in God in ways that could exasperate the most patient among us.

A church member once said with a smile, "That Sophia can drive me a little crazy sometimes!"

I said, "Yes. She can drive you crazy. But she is our crazy. She is one of us. We drive her crazy too. And certainly, we all drive God crazy together. But after all these years, we love her and accept her for who she is, just as she has accepted us for what we are."

Sophia died far younger than any of us could have ever predicted. She was such a force of nature, it seemed odd that she could die. When I looked at the faces of those who came to her memorial service, some were people who at one time or another found Sophia frustrating. All of us, however, grieved. We all shared a deep and abiding love for Sophia. We were grateful for the ways she taught us to value new people in our community and to work together in the love of Christ. In many ways, Sophia was one of the key reasons our church now includes people from India, Pakistan, South and Central America, and Africa. We now believe that until our church resembles the diversity of our elementary school classrooms, our love will be limited and our church will not fully reflect God's will.

INTENTIONAL INVITATION TO EXPAND YOUR CIRCLES

Research shows that our brains are like my Aunt Ibbie's table. We only have so many chairs to go around. The magic number may be 150. That is the number of relationships Dr. Robin Dunbar says the average human being can sustain at any given time. Dr. Dunbar is a professor of evolutionary psychology at the University of Oxford. He studied the social groupings of monkeys, apes, and humans. Humans consistently had about 150 relationships in their social groupings. Dunbar then looked at the usage of Facebook and found that the average person has about 150 friends. He even studied Christmas card networks. Most people don't send 150 Christmas cards. When you count how many total people are in the households who receive the Christmas cards, guess how many they reach? 150.

That is why 150 is called "Dunbar's Number."[5]

Dunbar says that we average about 150 relationships for two reasons. The first is the size of our brains. In particular, it is the size of the portion of your brain that handles social interactions. The larger the brain, the larger your group. This explains why mosquitos are always buzzing around trying to get your attention but never invest in the relationship. Time is the other big reason that 150 seems to be the magic number when it comes to relationships. Our brains are only so large, and our day is only so long. Relationships require us to allocate time, and the closer the relationship, the more time it will take. It turns out that the idea that we can have quality time—brief but unusually special moments shared with those closest to us—is a bit of a myth. Quality time actually requires a quantity of time so that you can enjoy a conversation or do something together. In each successive circle of relationships, you will spend less time and less energy. After the first 150, there is simply not much of you left over.[6]

Your pool of acquaintances far exceeds your 150 relationships. Many people can put a name with a face to over 1,500 people. But that is different from your active relationships and quite different from the people you would feel close enough to invite to a dinner in your home.

Dunbar's number describes our capacity and makes it important for us to think about the ways Christ's expansive love can work in our lives. Our stretching may be more in membership than quantity. Try something interesting. Write down the names of the five relationships in your innermost circle. These are those closest to you. These people not only know your most embarrassing moment, they were probably there when it happened. They would drive 200 miles at 2 a.m. if you needed them.

Then write the names of next ten people. These are close friends. You may not feel like you can call them for help at 2 a.m., but wouldn't hesitate at 2 p.m.

Do some circle analysis. How many of those names represent someone of a different ethnicity, socioeconomic status, political or religious belief? How many are significantly younger or older than you? Are your circles primarily homogeneous or heterogeneous groupings?

Now consider the names of the next twenty people in that third relational circle. If you were having a cookout on Labor Day, these people might be invited. How do your groupings in this circle compare to the first two? In considering Christ's intentional invitations extended in the calling of the disciples, are there any names in this circle that might move more inward on your graphic? Finally, think of your last circle. It will have 115 names. What names might go here?

One hundred fifty. That is about all our relationship baskets can hold. Take a look at the names you have written down. What do you notice about the list? Who are these people? Where did you meet them? Why are they important to you? How much variety is there among these names in terms of where they live, where they come from, race, religious practice, identity, culture, or political ideology? Do you see more variance in your inner, middle, or outer circles? In completing this exercise, many people find that their innermost circles are the most homogeneous. For some people, the whole list is similar.

Like the disciples, we may find that learning to love God with our heart, soul, mind, and strength, and loving our neighbors as ourselves involves opening our circles up to people Jesus wants us to meet. God will delight in putting people in your life unlike anyone you have ever known in the past. Embrace the instruction to love your neighbor as yourself, and you will care about them. Jesus has a way of bringing people into your life that you never expected and would have never chosen on your own.

As Jesus constantly expands our circle, we learn to truly love our neighbors as ourselves. Our joy is not in finding people we think are just like us, but in the authenticity of love expressed for any and all of God's children. Christ asks us to leave the preconditions that limit love behind. As we grow love, we drop our conditions related to who is in and who is out. Jesus is taking his first disciples on an expansive journey to learn how to love God and their neighbors. He doesn't tell them who else is going to be in his group and he doesn't tell them where they are going. Instead, he facilitates encounters, which continue to expand their love further and further. The same is true of us when we start our journey with Christ. Jesus doesn't tell you where you are going or who you will have to love. If you had that information, you might never take the journey. But without those companions, and without that journey, we will never become the people God intended us to be. We can learn to love the Lord our God with all our hearts, mind, souls, and strength, and love our neighbors as ourselves.

Of course, it may be a bit of a wild ride.

CHAPTER 3
LAVISH LOVE

The true meaning of love one's neighbor is not that it is a command from God which we are to fulfill, but that through it and in it we meet God.[1]

Martin Buber

I was in line to go through a security checkpoint at a large airport recently. It was crowded. A long line of travelers followed the path laid out by the retractable belts and stanchions. Everyone was in a rush. No one was going anywhere fast. In front of me was a set of parents with their two daughters. I guessed that one was four and the other was about six. The older one could not leave her sister alone. She would grab the hood on her sister's jacket and pull it over her head. The younger sister would put it down. The older sister would put it back up. The younger sister would protest and pull it down. The older sister would pull it back up. The younger sister retreated between her parents. The older sister stepped around them, came from behind, and now pulled the hood down. The younger sister responded by snarling and abruptly pulled the hood up again.

Things were calm for few minutes while both girls took a few steps as the line moved forward. They talked to their parents or looked at the people around them. Just when I thought harmony had been found, the younger girl quietly pushed her suitcase into her sister's bag, causing it to move to one side. Thus began the great suitcase territory war. Each girl would tap the other's suitcase and move it about an inch at a time. I was in that line for about 30 minutes, fascinated at the ingenuity of these girls to invent ever new ways to irritate each other. It was obvious that this was a pattern in their relationship. Neither cried or yelled. They did not disturb others, but they picked on each other with abandon the majority of time I observed them. I was working on this book at that time. As I watched, I took out a small notebook and wrote, "What would the world be like if people invested their creativity and energy in love?"

All people are born in the image of God. We are, as the Bible says, "fearfully and wonderfully made" (Psalm 139:14). The goodness of God is within us, but you don't have to spend much time with children to see that we sometimes struggle to let it out. When they get bored or in a bad mood, kids sometimes like to frustrate and generally bother other people until a sibling or a nearby child reaches the boiling point. Watching those sisters in the airport, I realized that I was not witnessing a sibling issue or child problem. I was observing the human condition. The sheer joy they received from their struggle to gain the upper hand was something that I absolutely understood.

All God's children have to be taught how to love. The time Jesus spent with his disciples provided them with the basic training they would need to lead others to follow him after his resurrection. Jesus expressed the core of his teaching when he spoke about a different way of life that was found in what he called the "kingdom of God." He used this phrase to help people understand that the way his followers were to live was very different from the way they had lived before they met him. No matter what they were in the past, whether fishermen, tax collectors, zealots, or any other profession or ideology, as his followers they were now to live by the standards of the kingdom of God. Following Jesus meant that they were accepting a new citizenship in a new life.

The Sermon on the Plain is Luke's shorter version of Matthew's Sermon on the Mount. In Luke's Gospel it immediately follows the account of Jesus' call to his disciples and the list of their names. The Sermon on the Plain is an orientation lecture from the rabbi to his disciples on the nature of God's love that they are expected to exhibit. It defines the norms of the conduct that citizens of God's kingdom will practice in their life together and as they encounter the larger world. The most common topic in the sermon is love. One wonders what the disciples thought when they heard Jesus' expectations for them. Jesus sets the bar rather high when he opens with, "I say to you that listen, Love your enemies, do good to those who hate you, bless those who curse you, pray for those who abuse you" (Luke 6:27-28).

It is only uphill from there. He tells his disciples to pray for those who hurt them, and give to those who request it. Just when the disciples were wondering if they heard him correctly, he reiterates, "Love your enemies, do good, and lend, expecting nothing in return" (Luke 6:35a).

Given the diverse backgrounds from which the first disciples came, one can see why they would benefit from an orientation session before they got too far down the road. But what a shock it must have been to hear Jesus tell them that they would be expected to be as compassionate as God, who is kind to the appreciative and the ungrateful alike. He tells them that they will no longer be allowed to judge others or criticize them or speak words of contempt about anyone. If they held a grudge against someone, or if there was an old wound that they were nursing for years, it was time to forgive and get on with life. Unless they forgave others, they would not be forgiven themselves.

Generosity in all things is the expectation of this new life. They are to stop worrying about fixing other people's problems or giving other people advice about how to be better or do better. They are to take a good look at their own lives and see if they are producing the fruit that a tree God planted would normally produce. If the fruit of their lives is all brambles and thorns, they are expected to call it evil and ask God for help. The reason Jesus focused their attention this way is that he wanted them to understand that if they were going to follow him, they were going to learn to be the most loving people on the planet. No other rabbi ever called a group of disciples to exhibit love in word and deed the way Jesus did.

PEOPLE REALLY DO THIS

Jesus' teaching is still relevant after two millennia because every generation has the opportunity to increase its capacity to love. When you read the Sermon on the Plain, you quickly realize that we are in as much need of an orientation to principles and practices of the kingdom of God as the first disciples. We live in a time when love sometimes feels like it is in limited supply. Since Cain first felt the jealousy that led him to hurt his brother, humans have found it easier to tear down rather than build up. Rather than learn from hurts and cruelty of the past, we seem stuck in a cycle. The victims may change over time, but the predictable pattern of struggle for dominance and power, along with the accompanying willingness to harm or exploit others carries forward. God understands our great need for teaching and example to overcome ourselves. We have the word and life of the incarnate Christ to guide us. It seems that a review of the inflicted hardships of human history could teach us a better way, but we do not seem able to absorb its lessons. There are people in this world who want to cling to the old ways. They do not believe in the love that Christ describes. Like love, hate often begins small, but if fed and nurtured, it will grow considerably.

That was true of the gunman who walked into the Tree of Life Synagogue in Pittsburgh's affluent Squirrel Hill neighborhood on a Saturday morning in October 2018 as services were beginning. He shouted anti-Semitic epithets and started shooting. Soon eleven people were dead. The shooter was later wounded by the police. When he arrived in the emergency room, he was still shouting, "I want to kill all the Jews."

Understanding the motivation for such a heinous act is difficult. This man was convinced by unfounded conspiracy theories on the Internet that Jewish people are trying to harm our country by assisting immigrants. He hoped to unleash a mudslide of hate. If you have ever seen live footage of a mudslide, you know that it begins with a small part of a rain-soaked hillside coming loose. On its own, this would not be dangerous. However, as it separates, it sets off a chain reaction down the hill. The earth is unstable, and as one sections slips away, more and more mud shakes loose beneath it and joins the rush downward. Picking up both volume and speed, the slide begins to destabilize more and more of the mountainside. It is fast, violent, and unstoppable. It covers or destroys everything in its path.

The shooter at the Tree of Life Synagogue hoped to do something similar. He hoped his action would break loose an avalanche of hate and violence toward his victims. He wanted others to follow his example so that more lives would be destroyed. By feeding and growing sentiments in his own heart, he felt justified in his actions to wound and kill others. The hate expressed was not in response to the actions of a group of people. It was the culmination of hate he planted and cultivated over the years. He no longer recognized that those he sought to harm were fellow children of God.

We do not like to think we have anything in common with a murderer.

However, anger, contempt, and hatred are all common to the human experience and all have this same dynamic. They start small, with a sentence spoken with irritation, a poorly chosen word, or a racial slur offered in the form of humor. Soon one thing leads to another and a relationship is damaged, a child no longer respects a parent in the same way, or people feel angry or fearful of what will come next. An extremist like this shooter hopes to unleash deadly violence. This is what Jesus tells his disciples they will have to remove from their lives.

By contrast, Jesus first calls his followers to do no harm. They are to grow their capacity to love to such an extent that there is no room left in their lives for anger, contempt, and hate. He tells his followers that they must release intentions to retaliate when unkindness and animosity are on the move. No longer are they to demand an eye for an eye, or wish for revenge. If you are a victim, you can seek justice. However, you are not to act in anger in order to wound others. According to Jesus, it is not a big accomplishment to love those who love you. Most people do that. The sign that God is claiming your life, and that you love God deeply, is your willingness to extend the mercy God has offered you to others.

It may seem impossible to act this way. Yet, people do. After the Pittsburgh shooter was wounded by law enforcement officials, he was taken to Allegheny General Hospital, where he received care. The president of that hospital, Dr. Jeff Cohen, lives down the street from the synagogue. Dr. Cohen heard the gunshots and chaos in his neighborhood that morning. That had to be on his mind when he entered the gunman's hospital room. Dr. Cohen went there not to express his outrage, or tell the man about the friends he lost that day. Dr. Cohen went to simply make sure this man received good care and was not in pain.

"I thought it was important to at least talk to him and meet him," Cohen said. "You can't on one hand say we should talk to each other, and then I don't talk to him. So you lead by example, and I'm the leader of the hospital."

When Dr. Cohen left the room, the FBI agent that was guarding the gunman said, "I don't know that I could have done that."

Why did Dr. Cohen do that?

Dr. Cohen is a member of the Tree of Life Synagogue. He was nurtured in the Jewish faith and raised to be kind and compassionate. You can hear that in his response to the reporters that day about the role of the hospital and its staff. "We're not here to judge you. We're not here to ask 'Do you have insurance?' or 'Do you not have insurance?' We're here to take care of people that need our help."

Dr. Cohen also said that he was also inspired by the words of grace that members of Emanuel AME Church shared when they spoke of forgiveness to a white supremacist after he killed their family and church members in South Carolina.[2] The young white man who was charged with murder after the massacre in the historic black church in Charleston in 2015 stood with a vacant look at the court hearing. He showed no sign of remorse or repentance. Relatives of the nine who were murdered were given the opportunity to address him one by one. Their words were often mixed with grief and anger. Several of those who spoke offered him forgiveness.

"I acknowledge that I am very angry," said Bethane Middleton Brown, who said her slain sister, DePayne Middleton Doctor, would have urged love. "She taught me that we are the family that love built," Middleton Brown said. "We have no room for hating, so we have to forgive."[3]

LOVE COVERS A MULTITUDE OF SINS

These church members and relatives offer forgiveness after losing so much because they are simply obedient to the call of Christ's love. This is a remarkable act of faith that helps us resize and reconsider the hurt and anger we hold on to for much smaller offenses. Jesus' call to this level of persistent love is reiterated later in the teaching found in 1 Peter, "Above all, maintain constant love for one another, for love covers a multitude of sins" (1 Peter 4:8).

Here the author of 1 Peter calls us to value each other so deeply that we maintain a constant love for one another. Imagine what your life would be like if you held a constant love in your relationships and community. Such a life sounds ideal, and yet, when we think further, a bit daunting. We have a lot of reasons why we are not constant in the love that we fail to maintain. It may be because we are dealing with people. It would be much easier to love people if people did not act like people. By contrast, it is easy to love our dog Mudge. When we enter the house, he is 85 pounds of tail-wagging, I'm-so-excited-to-see-you hospitality. Mudge is so overcome with the desire to show his affection by licking our hands and faces that he had to teach himself to put a chew toy in his mouth so that he could control himself. Even so, he maintains a ritual of walking in circles around each new person who enters our home while his tail slaps the wall, doorframe, furniture, and anything else in its path.

If people greeted you this way when you entered your home or office, it would be pretty easy to love them too. But when your child doesn't return your text messages, even though you pay for their phone and phone service, a love failure can occur. When your coworker doesn't meet the deadlines required by the contract you are working on, even after they asked to be placed on the project, it can be hard to maintain a constant love. When a friend writes charged political views on their social media page that speak in contempt of the views you hold, you can wonder if you really know that person at all. People can be hard.

We can be hard too. Our moods and temperament get in our own way as well. Put us under stress, deprive us of sleep or simply catch us in a bad moment, and we undermine our desire to love others with constancy. Circumstances add another dimension of complexity. The family who is being evacuated from a coastal area due to a hurricane, cutting their long-anticipated vacation three days short, may find themselves sullen and impatient on the way home. (In truth, I was the only one who was sullen and impatient. My wife and kids were fine. But you get the idea.)

The call to constant love means that we are going to need Jesus, not just to set the standard for us, but to work in our lives. We are going to need to ask Jesus to help us see the world and its people as he sees them, and love as he loves. We will need to cultivate practices that keep us connected to Christ, so that we can actually follow the standard he sets in the Sermon on the Plain, along with the rest of his teaching and the life we witness in the Gospels. This dependence on Christ is exactly what he had in mind. Only when we learn to yield and ask him to exercise lordship over our lives will we be able to love our neighbors as ourselves. His lordship will provide greater guidance and command over our moods, responses to others or reactions to the news outlets we watch, listen to, or read. If we are to truly love others, we need Jesus to become "Lord of all" rather than the focus of one hour on Sunday. Learning to love our neighbor transforms us into the people God longs for us to be. It is in this way that "love covers a multitude of sins." It is what makes maintaining a "constant" love for others possible.

MORE THAN ONE MEANING

Given what we understand about our humanity, Jesus' call to constant love could be understood as a call to lavish love. Just as the fullness of God's love has been freely, generously, and unconditionally poured out upon us, so are we called to lavish love and offer it freely, generously, and without condition. The word *lavish* can be used as a verb or an adjective. Merriam-Webster defines *lavish* as "expending or bestowing profusely . . . marked by profusion or excess; to bestow something in generous or extravagant unmeasured quantities."

When we lavish love, we offer it freely and generously, the same way that God loves us and offers us grace and forgiveness when we ask for it. When we offer a lavish love, we offer love in abundance. Jesus asks us to lavish a lavish love. The more we love others, the more love changes our actions, our words, our character, and our lives. Before we knew Jesus, we really didn't have that much motivation to love others "lavishly." We were not beings void of love. We loved, but we exchanged units of love with those who repaid us in kind, as though it could be stored in a love bank account and withdrawn at will. We did not consider love to be a full-time job, a "constant" call on our lives. Our love was more like a side hustle. Some days we didn't even show up to work. It was catch as catch can.

Then we discovered that Jesus died to destroy the power that sin and evil had over us. Through his resurrection, we realized that Jesus had the power to give us new life and enable us to overcome the habits that hurt us. This new life in Christ is an opportunity for the love of God to live in us and through us. In so doing, we experience the rising tide of Christ's love in our lives. It covers and then washes away our sins and fills us with the desire to love God and our neighbor.

With this experience with Christ, we discover we too can love lavishly, and that love covers a multitude of sins in the world. We discover that the more we forgive others, the more love fills our hearts and crowds out old hurts and resentments. More and more sin's power over us is repealed and the power of love is displayed. While it is sometimes unwise to drop all boundaries with someone who may hurt us again, lavish love allows us to forgive a person from a distance so that we no longer feel anger or contempt or repetitively re-experience our wound on the movie screen in our mind. Jesus' call to forgive overcomes the injury and helps us heal. Love lavishly and we are not tempted to use words of contempt or spread unkind stories about another person. This call to constant love is not a dreamer's verse. It is a description of what it means to follow Christ and live out the lavish love he told his disciples would be the basis and norm of their new life.

HOW DO WE DO THIS?

Author Eddie Pipkin talks about a visit to Longwood Gardens outside Philadelphia. He writes, "I was perusing the bonsai exhibit, enchanted by (a) diminutive crape myrtle. . . .I knew that the art and technique of bonsai was based on patience and a meticulous attention to detail. [This tree] first became a part of their collection in *1944!* While World War II was still raging, it began its 'training,' as they say in bonsai circles: horticulturists lovingly tended every branch and bloom, pruning with great care and deciding with careful thought which branches would grow strong. They thought decades ahead as to what form the mature tree would take, and the result is a living masterpiece of beauty and form."[4]

A picture of this small tree shows its remarkable shape and beauty. Much happened over time to give it such a perfect form. One master gardener after another took up the task of pruning and supporting the tree in its growth. The beauty of that tree was not an accident. Even odd twists of the trunk or imperfections that might have damaged it were nurtured in such a way as to add character and distinction to the tree.

An essential practice of those who care for a bonsai tree is observation. The gardener spends time with the tree, looking at its growth and where growth has been hindered. By observing the life of the tree over time, the gardener knows how to best shape and form the tree so that it can express its full beauty.

OBSERVE

Observe your life for a moment. Take a look at yourself as though you are staring in a mirror. The art and beauty of you also rely on patience and meticulous attention to detail. I don't mean your physical appearance. I am speaking of the beauty of your life. You have become the person you are because of thousands of small decisions, the best of which you made after prayer and thought of the will of God. Like a bonsai tree that has been slowly fashioned for many years, careful thought has gone into your life as well. God created you. Throughout your life, other people have cared for you. Think about the people that you met who helped you become a better person. Recall the teachers who invested in you, the family members who supported you and the many people who showed up at just the right time to help you. As you grew older talents, abilities, and interest in sports, clubs, and contests were displayed. You may have joined the military where you received intense physical and skills training. You may have entered an apprenticeship at a job or went to college. As the years passed by, you became, and perhaps with intentionality gave thought to, what form the mature you would take. The result is the person you are today.

Notice that some of your most interesting attributes are not outcomes of decisions you made. They are present because of what God infused into your life from the very beginning. Your life is unique. It holds certain abilities, certain superpowers present from the very beginning as you were formed in the image of God. You uniquely bless the world. Lavish love calls us to examine our own lives so we can identify all the ways God, as the master gardener, both supported and pruned us so that we could become the people we are today.

GIVE THANKS

An unobserved life often leads to an ungrateful life. That is true anywhere. It is easy to forget the benefits of a job, isn't it? "I work so hard. The hours are so numerous. The clients are so demanding." Keep thinking like that and soon you forget that a monthly salary is deposited in your bank account and when you were sick, you had days of paid leave that you used.

I think the author of Psalm 103 practiced observation. I can picture the psalmist observing his life and feeling an overwhelming desire to express thanksgiving and exaltation to God:

Bless the LORD, O my soul,
    and all that is within me,
    bless his holy name.
Bless the LORD, O my soul,
    and do not forget all his benefits.

Psalm 103:1-2

It is easy to forget the benefits of so many things: family, marriage, parents, children, citizenship, and church. When the author of Psalm 103 looked in the mirror to observe his life, he remembered the benefits of his relationship with God. The psalmist recalled times when he needed forgiveness and the Lord offered it or someone who also loved the Lord extended it. The author could recall times when God "redeems your life from the Pit" (103:4).

When we take time to consider the wider perspective of our personal histories, when we contemplate all the ways God has loved and blessed us, our hearts cannot help but overflow with thanksgiving and praise. The psalmist is wise to speak directly to the soul and instruct it not to forget all of God's benefits. Just as we benefit from taking time to observe and reflect, so our lives grow in satisfaction and fulfillment when we give thanks for the ways that God's love has been shown in our lives. As we name and count our blessings we experience a growing desire to love and bless others. It becomes more natural to love the God who first loved us with all our heart, mind, soul, and strength, and to love our neighbors as ourselves. Lavish love no longer sounds so far-fetched. Giving thanks for the love of God throughout your life is a necessary practice because a strong love is never possible with a weak memory.

A heart of gratitude allows safety in recalling dark times as well as those that were bright. Can you recall times when it felt like you were in a deep hole? While we would not wish those times on anyone else, we find that we can still feel gratitude. In those circumstances we felt the presence of the

Holy Spirit. It was powerful because we realized that we were not alone. Perhaps the Lord used people around you to lift you up, or something that happened was a sign that God was with you. It is powerful to sing the familiar refrain, "I once was lost but now I'm found," because we can recall how that was true in our lives and exalt the Lord with praise and thanksgiving as a result.

LAVISH LOVE

One of the most important observations the psalmist makes has to do with the nature of God's love. God is named as the one "who crowns you with steadfast love and mercy" (103:4). The word for love in the Hebrew is *hesed*. It speaks of the constant love of the Lord. We know the constant love Christ calls us to, because we have experienced it. We may struggle to remember the Lord, but the Almighty never forgets us. The psalmist goes on to capture God's *hesed* for each of us,

> The LORD is merciful and gracious,
>> slow to anger and abounding in steadfast love.
>>>> Psalm 103:8

When we observe and remember the deep love of God for us, our hearts overflow with thanksgiving that is expressed not only in words but in our love of others. We are thankful to our Creator for everything in the world, but most especially for loving us. When we know how much God loves us, we cannot help loving God in return. Loving God forms a benevolent heart toward others because we know of God's love for them. *Benevolence* means having a "good will" toward all those around us. We wish the best for them, and we act in ways that promote their well-being. Carrying out benevolence means "first, doing nothing harmful, and second, doing all that we can to be useful."[5] The strength created by the gratitude I feel for what I see the Lord has done, leads to a benevolence that I share with others.

Benevolence changes how we see each other. Once we see God's love in our lives, it impacts how we love others. Jewish philosopher Martin Buber's understanding of human relationships, found in his book *I and Thou*, is helpful. Buber said that we can relate to others either by experience or encounter. When we relate to someone as an experience, it is an "I-It" moment. One person is the subject, the other is an object. Most of our interactions with other humans are I-It interactions because they are transactional in nature.[6] Imagine you are at an airport. There is a shuttle driver who takes you to your hotel. You hand him your bags. While he drives to the airport, you look at e-mail on your phone, trying to catch up. He listens to the radio. When he drops you off he hands you your bags. You pay him and include a tip. That is a transactional experience. To classify this as an "I-It" experience does not mean that it is bad. Most interactions we have with others are transactional in nature as we go to the store, pay for childcare, receive paychecks at work, or make an appointment for some service in the future. Our society is designed for such interactions. Even more of our interactions with others are I-It experiences as e-mail and social media are present on our handheld devices.

For instance, imagine the same scenario. Again, you are at the airport. The driver shows up and puts your bags in the trunk. This time, however, the battery on your phone is dead. Rather than look at your e-mail, you strike up a conversation. You ask the driver how long he has lived in this city. You follow this with a number of other questions about what he enjoys about driving, other jobs he has worked, his family, and what he enjoys about his life. Soon you are really talking. He shares that this is a second job. He is also a sales manager for a beverage company. He works this job so that his wife can get her master's degree while their daughter also goes to college. You learn that his name is Davis and that he has a son from a previous marriage who lives in another city. After a period of estrangement, he was able to make contact with his son, who shared that he is gay. You ask Davis how he feels about that, and he shares how sad it made him that his son thought this information would anger him or change the love that he feels for his son. By the time Davis pulls into the hotel, you have offered to pray for him during the coming week as he plans to reach out to his son again. You thank each other for the conversation, and you feel something unusual. You have only known him for about thirty minutes, but you sense that you will miss Davis when he pulls away.

Martin Buber would call this an "I-Thou" encounter. The conversation was relational. Here you turned toward the driver by asking questions about his life. You learned his name. As you asked these questions, the driver became the person, Davis, who began to trust that he could disclose important parts of his life to you. You understood that the stories he shared of his past, and the information he offers about his family, are sacred to him. You honored that by the way you listened and spoke to him. As you walk into your hotel, you are left with the hope that Davis and his son will find a way to love each other in a relationship that will include honesty and mutual support. Because you turned toward Davis in this conversation, you find that you are changed. Your mood is more thoughtful and positive. You look at the faces around you and wonder what burdens they bear, or what joys they celebrate today. The care you showed in your response turns this encounter into one that can be described as love. You have experienced the expression of you that God desires. You realize how much God loves you because you like this you. This is the you you want to be. Walking into the hotel, you experience a desire, an excitement, an anticipation of living into Christ's call to lavish, constant love.

After the Squirrel Hill synagogue shooting, I contacted Rabbi Michael Holzman, who serves a synagogue in our area. Rabbi Holzman is a friend, and our congregations work together in an interfaith community organization. I was worried about him. I knew that the man who murdered the members of the Tree of Life Synagogue wanted to send grief, fear, and harm into all synagogues and other houses of worship as well. People who practice hate hope to diminish the lives of others.

Love is a powerful force much needed in the world. It creates the stability that keeps the mudslide of anger or violence from breaking loose. Love overcomes a multitude of sins. Rabbi Holzman invited faith communities in our area to join the Northern Virginia Hebrew Congregation for their Friday evening Shabbat service. It rained hard that night, and I wondered how many people would come. As I pulled into the parking lot, I realized that the rain was not deterring anyone's attendance. Those who love treat others with decency, respect, and sacred worth, regardless of rain. Hundreds of people came. Many had to drive away as parking had been exceeded beyond capacity. I was so glad that so many members of Floris United Methodist Church, where I serve, were present. Seated on the bema were pastors of a variety of churches. There were leaders of local mosques. There were politicians from both parties. There were clergy from a variety of races and cultures.

The Shabbat service was powerful, even though a great deal of it was in Hebrew. People were smiling. Representatives of various faith communities took turns participating, reading Scripture, prayers, or other readings. Listening to the Scripture and prayers, hearing the words of Rabbi Holzman as he encouraged his congregation and welcomed the community that night, I could feel the presence of God in our mutual concern for one another. Members of the synagogue approached me at the end of the service and said, "It just means so much to us that you are here." I realized that it meant so much to me too. Lavish love fell down on us like the rain that beat down on the roof of the synagogue.

Where there is love and community, fear diminishes. That is true in our personal lives and that is true in our life together in our society. "Above all, maintain constant love for one another, for love covers a multitude of sins" (1 Peter 4:8). One can see why Jesus insisted without exception that his disciples learn to place their love of God and love of others as the key priority of their lives. The closing prayer of the Shabbat service that was shared that night was the *Hashiveinu*, which means "Protect Us." It is a worthy prayer for those who follow Christ, who want to actually keep his command to offer a lavish love to the world.

Let there be love and understanding among us.
Let peace and friendships be our shelter from life's storms.
Adonai, help us to walk with good companions,
to live with hope in our hearts and eternity in our thoughts,
that we may lie down and rise up waiting to do Your will.

As I read that prayer, I thought of Jesus teaching in the Sermon on the Plain: "I say to you that listen, Love your enemies, do good to those who hate you, bless those who curse you, pray for those who abuse you" (Luke 6:27-28).

It is far more likely that we will be able to actually do such difficult things if we are in the flow of God's love and the company of good companions, who help keep hope alive in our hearts and nurture the desire to do God's will.

CHAPTER 4
OPENHEARTED LOVE

Travel is fatal to prejudice, bigotry, and narrow-minded-
ness and many of our people need it sorely on these
accounts. Broad, wholesome, charitable views of men
and things cannot be acquired by vegetating in one little
corner of the earth all one's lifetime.[1]

Mark Twain

When you live near Washington, D.C., you have a lot of options if you want to see a museum, monument, or place of historic importance. One of my favorites is a less-visited site in the historic neighborhood of Anacostia in the southeast quadrant of the District of Columbia. It is the home of Frederick Douglass. Douglass is an American hero. He was born a slave and taught himself to read and write, something the state of Maryland at that time considered a crime that could have been punished by death. Working with Anne Murray, a free black woman who would become his wife, Douglass escaped slavery and gained his freedom. He joined northern abolitionists and became an admired speaker who drew large crowds.

Despite his lack of formal education, Douglass was so eloquent that some doubted he had ever been a slave. His years in bondage, however, enabled him to vividly describe the harm done to black men, women, and children who worked farms and plantations and kept the homes of the whites who enslaved them. Douglass lived a remarkable life. He published three books about his life and a popular newspaper to advance the abolitionist movement. His prominence and wealth grew. He consulted with President Lincoln on the use of black army troops for the first time in combat during the Civil War, lobbied for fair pay for these men, called for voting rights for black men, and argued for women's suffrage.

Frederick Douglass knew what it was like to live as an enslaved man in a country that perpetuated an institution of grave injustice. His drive for justice grew out of a desire to right wrongs. He believed that his work honored God and was a form of true Christianity. Douglass wrote about the hypocrisy of Christians who supported slavery:

> I therefore hate the corrupt, slaveholding, women-whipping, cradle-plundering, partial and hypocritical Christianity of this land.... I look upon it as the climax of all misnomers, the boldest of all frauds, and the grossest of all libels.... I am filled with unutterable loathing when I contemplate the religious pomp and show, together with the horrible inconsistencies, which everywhere surround me. We have men-stealers for ministers, women-whippers for missionaries, and cradle-plunderers for church members. The man who wields the blood-clotted cowskin during the week fills the pulpit on Sunday, and claims to be a minister of the meek and lowly Jesus.... The slave auctioneer's bell and the church-going bell chime in with each other, and the bitter cries of the heart-broken slave are drowned in the religious shouts of his pious master.[2]

Douglass called out the sins of his time because he was the kind of person who didn't just pray, "thy kingdom come, thy will be done on earth as it is in heaven," only to wait for some celestial magic to take effect. He believed that God called him to work for God's will in the world. As a Christian, he could not understand how other Christians could be content in a world where the kingdom of God was a concept rather than a reality.

Douglass created friction everywhere he went, even at home. After his wife of forty-four years, Anne Murray Douglass, died, he began spending time with Helen Pitts, whom he married in 1884. Helen had worked with him in the suffrage movement and served as his secretary. She was also white, and the marriage created tension with his children. Douglass argued that if he didn't marry Helen "just because she happens to be white," he would be a "moral coward."[3]

I visited Cedar Hill, the Douglass home, with my family. We watched the short biographical video shown by the National Park Service before the tour. In the final scene, an elderly Frederick Douglass comes home on what will be the last day of his life. A young black man waits for him and asks him for advice. Douglass repeated one word, which seems to sum up his life's work, three times: "Agitate. Agitate. Agitate."

When I heard that word, I thought of how white people must have viewed Douglass. Rarely do those whose life work is to agitate find themselves adored by the general public. Those in power, as well as the average person in the broader society, typically find the one who agitates to be nothing but trouble. As the film ended, I thought of how exhausting that must have been for Douglass. Our group walked up the hill and entered the house. We moved from room to room while the ranger offered us information about Douglass's life and work. On the back of the house, Douglass added a washroom, something that was rather modern in the 1880's. Our guide picked up an antique tool from a basin. It looked like a plunger, but had a conical end made of metal rather than rubber. "Does anyone know what this is?" she asked. "An agitator," called out a member of our group. "That is right!" she said happily. "This is what you used to make sure your clothes come out clean and fresh. You use this to agitate the water and the laundry so that the soap can clean the fabric."

AGITATE

I had never seen *agitate* from those two perspectives. Used one way I see the fiery Douglass confronting injustice and disturbing the status quo. Used another, I observe Douglass as he works to cleanse the soul of the nation from the stains of slavery and inequality to bring the beauty of justice to the fabric of our society. To be agitated is to have our lives cleansed of what inhibits God's love from radiating from our lives. The grime of prejudice and injustice is something to which a person grows accustomed and does not notice, but which others observe readily when present. Frederick Douglass could see it on the abusive slaveowners who faithfully attended church every week. Likewise, people today can see and hear the way we think and behave toward groups of people based on their color, culture, or country of origin.

When Jesus began his journey with his disciples, he understood that if they were going to love others, they needed to go through a long process of agitation. There are two essential areas that Jesus agitates and hopes to clean up—the way his followers see gender and race. These two areas are foundational if we are to expand our relational circles and fulfill the command to love God and our neighbor as ourselves. Jesus was an experiential teacher. To work in these two key areas, he took his disciples on a journey where they encountered people and situations that confronted their most deeply held beliefs and biases about other people. Rabbinic students do not challenge their teachers. They get close to them. They observe. They listen. They follow the pattern of their rabbi's behaviors and actions. Disciples hope to so consistently follow the example of their rabbi that anyone observing them will see more of the rabbi and less of the disciple. As they do this, they let their old ways of interacting with the world die so that the lessons of the rabbi can flourish within them and give them new life.

Experiences that change the way we look at the world or people, however, are not always easy. Imagine how disoriented Jesus' male disciples were when he first allowed women to join their ranks.

> Soon afterwards he went on through cities and villages, proclaiming and bringing the good news of the kingdom of God. The twelve were with him, as well as some women who had been cured of evil spirits and infirmities: Mary, called Magdalene, from whom seven demons had gone out, and Joanna, the wife of Herod's steward Chuza, and Susanna, and many others, who provided for them out of their resources.
>
> Luke 8:1-3

We can assume that at the beginning of their journey most, if not all, of the twelve disciples reflected their culture and carried a neutral to negative view of women. Commentator Kenneth Bailey points out that while the Hebrew Bible offered stories of important women like Ruth, Esther, Deborah and Jael, and speaks honorably of women in Proverbs 31, there was also a great deal of negative teaching about women in Jewish culture at that time.[4] Ben Sirach, a scholar who lived in the second century BC, encouraged respect for women who were good wives and mothers. However, he also said that women should not be deeded property, were the source of unbearable spite and felt that having daughters was a misfortune. Bailey offers these words from Ben Sirach:

> Do not let her parade her beauty before any man,
> or spend her time among married women;
> for from garments comes the moth,
> and from a woman comes woman's wickedness.

73

> Better is the wickedness of a man than a woman who
> does good;
>> it is woman who brings shame and disgrace.
>> Ben Sirach 42:12-14

It makes you think that Ben Sirach possibly had a few unresolved childhood issues. While he does not speak for all Jewish scholars in his day, it is generally true that by the time of the New Testament, the position of women was inferior to that of men.[5] It is all the more remarkable that in this environment, Jesus had female disciples, who not only traveled with him and the guys, but also supported the movement out of their own means. These women were economically invested in Jesus' ministry. In other sections of the Gospels, the authors note that women were in the crowds listening to Jesus, or like Mary, sitting in with the men when he visited her home. Bailey emphasizes that Jesus breaks the cultural norms of both his religion and society by treating women as equal to men, something so unusual that the Gospel writers seem to want to make sure we will see it:

> To the one who had told him this, Jesus replied, "Who
> is my mother, and who are my brothers?" And *pointing
> to his disciples*, he said, "Here are *my mother and my
> brothers*! For whoever does the will of my Father in
> heaven is my brother and sister and mother."
>> Matthew 12:48-50, emphasis added

As Jesus accepts women along with men as his disciples, as he treats them the same, rather than requiring them to stand at a distance or only give the deep teaching to the men, Jesus agitates not only his male disciples, but anyone who observed his ministry. Like a pair of braces that slowly move teeth through persistent pressure, Jesus works to transform his disciples. He does this to change the assumptions we make about people based on their gender, just as he will challenge other factors like their race, culture, and religion. The journey the disciples took was an expedition into their deepest beliefs and biases about other people. They were forced to look at the assumptions they were given from the time of their childhoods, so that they could unlearn anything that conflicted with the governing principles of the kingdom of God.

One of the best examples of Jesus' commitment to agitate is the encounter he creates with the woman at the well in the Gospel of John. John tells us that "he left Judea and started back to Galilee. But he had to go through Samaria" (John 4:3-4). When I read that text, I want to say, "This is Jesus we are talking about. King of kings, Lord of lords. He doesn't have to do anything he does not want to do."

While it is true that the fastest way to get from Judea to Galilee is to travel directly through Samaria, Jewish people were known to take the long way. They would travel east, cross the Jordan River, and then travel north through Perea and the area known as the Decapolis, to Galilee. Jesus is very intentional, but he never seems to be in a hurry. It seems logical that he went through Samaria intentionally in order to agitate his disciples. Jesus knew that some, if not all, of his disciples had a closed heart toward the people of Samaria, whom they disliked and distrusted.

There was a five-hundred-year-old hostility between the people of the former Northern Kingdom of Israel and the people of the former Southern Kingdom of Judah. When the Assyrians conquered the Northern Kingdom in 722 BC, they deported many of the citizens and resettled people from other conquered territories in their place. Eventually these people intermarried with the remaining Israelites. As they combined households, they also combined religions. They accepted various gods and goddesses of these other cultures and set up a place of worship on Mount Gerizim so that they would no longer have to go to the Temple in Jerusalem. Jewish people of Jesus' time judged the people of Samaria to be idolaters, ceremonially unclean, and socially unsavory. Perhaps what frustrated them the most was the sense that Samaritans should know better. When your heart is closed to a whole race of people, you will go out of your way to avoid them, even if it means the long way home to Galilee.

But not Jesus. He goes right through Samaria and stops at a well in the Samaritan town of Sychar. While the disciples are otherwise occupied, Jesus meets a woman from the town who has come to fill her water jars. She agrees to give Jesus a drink, as he begins a conversation with her. Jesus is not great at small talk. He speaks to people about issues that are real and important. Before she knows it, they discuss her love life, her religion, and a bit of politics. Essentially Jesus feels free to discuss every topic you were taught to avoid with strangers. Before long Jesus has divulged that he is the Messiah. This is the kind of ground that he covers in a short conversation. When the disciples return, John tells us, "They were astonished that he was speaking with a woman, but no one said, 'What do you want?' or 'Why are you speaking with her?'" (John 4:27).

We may assume that the disciples have a way to go before they will reach Jesus' practice on gender equality. Not only is Jesus talking to a woman, but she is also a Samaritan. In that time, it was off-limits socially for a man to talk to an unaccompanied woman in a place where there were no witnesses. They were probably worried about accusations people could have made against Jesus. The fact that she is a Samaritan only adds to the discomfort. You can tell that they are being agitated by this encounter. They are bewildered by Jesus' actions, but they do not say anything to him.

UNEXPECTED DESTINATIONS

Much is written about this conversation with the woman at the well. She may be shunned by others because of the past and current relationships she has had with men. She seems to hope that Jesus is the Messiah, and goes to tell the people of her town. What few scholars discuss is what happens when the people of Sychar come to meet Jesus for themselves: "So when the Samaritans came to him, they asked him to stay with them; and he stayed there two days" (John 8:40).

Picture the faces of the disciples as Jesus accepts the invitation for all of them to stay in the homes of Samaritans for two days. This would require them to sleep in Samaritan beds, eat Samaritan food, drink Samaritan water, and talk to Samaritan people—for two straight days. This is not easy when you have grown up hearing about the dirty Samaritans who sold out their religion for a bunch of wooden and stone idols. They had undoubtedly heard that Mount Gerizim was a second-rate excuse for Mount Zion, the true center of Jewish worship in Jerusalem. As children the adults around them helped close their minds toward Samaritans by opinions they offered, jokes they told and examples of what Samaritans did and did not do that made them indecent and untrustworthy people. This is the base of knowledge that the disciples carried with them as they traveled in Samaria. I would love to have seen the look on the faces of the disciples when Jesus said, "Guess what? We get to stay with the Samaritans tonight!"

Jesus, by contrast, opens a doorway into the life of this Samaritan woman. He thinks and knows things about her history and context that the average man from Nazareth could have never identified or even considered. After you have read the Gospels a few times, familiarity with Jesus' life and teaching makes it easy to forget that he is both fully divine and fully human. Jesus comes to human interactions with an open heart and an open mind because he knows people fully. He is not limited by cultural bias. He is not constricted by prejudice. He is not boxed in by the stereotypes. There is nothing that closes him off to other people. This is why he is able to interact with them with deep love and honesty. He is able to understand where people have been wounded in life and what motivates their actions. He is able to see and call out human sin quickly, so that people can choose to transform. Jesus takes his disciples on a journey through unexpected places because he knows this persistent agitation can open even the most tightly closed of hearts.

I recall building a church in a Mexican village with its members and a group of teenagers from two churches where I was the pastor. My wife, Karen, and I led this group, most of whom had never traveled out of their home state, much less the country. Communication was limited, other than for a few who spoke some Spanish they learned in high school. That lack of communication skills helped turn everyone into keen observers. The only way to communicate was through simple acts of kindness, the desire to share the burden of the work and help each other throughout the day. As a result, great warmth and respect grew.

The students noticed the contrast between the lower standard of living of their hosts and the high degree of hospitality they offered to our group. While we were given mattresses in a bedroom at night, we soon realized that our host families were sleeping on the floor in another part of the house. Women worked all day without the help of appliances or electricity to produce a wonderful meal each night. The Mexican men and women who worked with us endured the heat without complaint. They worked longer, harder, and with greater skill than anyone in our group. They welcomed us as brothers and sisters in Christ and found ways to communicate joy and humor throughout the day, despite our language barrier. During a break from mixing cement on the roof in the scorching sun one afternoon, one young man said, "I thought people in Mexico took siestas every afternoon and kind of kicked back and avoided work the rest of the day. I'm trying to keep up and these guys are going to kill me with their pace!"

Everyone laughed at the absurdity of our industrious hosts calling for nap time. One by one, the students in our group began to share other negative impressions that they had been taught about people in Mexico by people in their life, the majority of whom had never even gone to Mexico. The pastor could have shared one hundred lessons on Mexican culture, the unfairness of racial bias, the unchristian nature of prejudice, and a host of other issues. Nothing helped our group see and respect Mexican people like being offered hospitality in their homes, building a church facility together, or eating meals with one another each day. The experience made us openhearted to each other as we found Christ in the midst of our time together.

OPENHEARTED LIVING

Jesus is trying to help us experience openhearted living. Closed hearts squelch our ability to love God and love our neighbor. If we believe that our neighbor is unworthy of our attention, someone to be treated as less than human or a person who cannot be trusted because of the color of their skin or the location of their birth, then we will never be able to honor the command to love. By making his followers stay in the Samaritan village, Jesus offers them the opportunity to encounter Samaritans as children of God. Something good must have happened. By the time they left, many in the town believed in Jesus as the Messiah, not based on what the woman said, but on their own encounter with the love of Jesus and his disciples.

Like the trip to Samaria or Mexico, so often what we think we know about people is based upon what we have heard or been told, rather than what we have observed or experienced. If you want to be a disciple of Jesus, you have to be ready to be agitated by the encounters the love of Christ will require of you. Jesus does not suggest that we love our neighbors. He commands it. Typically, we ask the same closed-hearted, love-limiting question posed by the lawyer recorded in the Gospel of Luke, "and who is my neighbor?" (10:29). In response, Jesus tells a story about a Samaritan who is good, a surprise to the crowd who held their stereotypes close and their prejudice closer, but no surprise to Jesus, who actually knew good Samaritans. Jesus knows that every person in the world is a child of God.

As the preexistent Christ, he knows that the Creator has given life, breath, and a soul to each one and values them all. They are all made in God's image.

As we receive God's love, so Jesus calls us to love others. Being open to others is a hallmark of Christian love, which is why genuine Christians care about people without thought to so many of the factors people consider when they see another person. Jesus calls us out of our comfort zones. He asks us to put down the multi-lens bias that gets in the way of our vision of others. Yet, for many, this is a very hard set of glasses to remove.

Throughout my lifetime, America has been a place of tension and conflict over issues of race and racial justice. A vivid reminder of the continued impact of the legacy of bigotry occurred in 2017, when an assortment of alt-right and neo-Nazi groups rallied in Charlottesville, Virginia, to protest the potential removal of Confederate monuments and names from a city square.[6] It was shocking to see a long line of torch-bearing men walk down the lawn of the University of Virginia campus to kick off the "Unite the Right" rally. The next day numerous acts of violence followed and culminated in the death of Heather Heyer, when a white supremacist drove his car into a group of counter-protesters.

This is a continuation of a conflict that has been present since the first colonists landed at Jamestown, displacing native tribes. Not much later, they brought enslaved African laborers to the shores of Virginia, my home state. Virginians have many reminders of a centuries-old struggle for racial justice. While the slave auction houses of Richmond were torn down many years ago, the White House of the Confederacy and the capitol building where General Robert E. Lee accepted his commission are well-preserved. You can visit plantations where enslaved people generated tremendous wealth for their white owners while being forced to live in destitute poverty without hope of economic advancement. In recent years these sites have demonstrated a commitment to interpret the history of slavery and talk about the hardships and injustices endured by enslaved people to produce the capital their white owners used to build personal and social affluence. Within seventy miles of my home there are thousands of acres of Civil War battlefields set aside to tell the story of the devastating struggle brought on by the commitment of southern states to uphold the institution of slavery.

One would think commitment to sharing this history would lead to a longing for equality and an active desire for justice in the current time. How could people live in a place with so many reminders of a tainted past and not want to see all people enjoy the fruits of a democratic society today? Yet, there are still Christians in Virginia and in other parts of the country who speak of the "lost cause" of the South, hold deep affection for the Confederate flag and its legacy, and do not speak out when African American people are put down, made the object of jokes or the targets of words of contempt. Such examples of prejudice are not just true in the southern states, but in other parts of the country and toward other groups of people as well.

A NEW CREATION

The old ways do not go away on their own. We have to be taught how to love. We have to choose love as a way of life. The call to a new way of life in the teaching of Christ is found throughout the New Testament by those who best understood the intentions of Jesus' ministry because they were so close in time to it. The Apostle Paul writes, "If anyone is in Christ, there is a new creation: everything old has passed away; see, everything has become new!" (2 Corinthians 5:17).

Paul understood that when we accept the forgiveness, love, and grace that Jesus extends to us in his sacrificial death, we also receive the new life he offers to us in his resurrection. What does it mean for us to be a new creation? It means that as we experience our salvation, our new start that is free from the bondage of past sins, we also enjoy Jesus' lordship. We no longer live from a worldly point of view. We love what Jesus loves, not what the world says is acceptable or to be admired. Like the first disciples, we must follow the rabbi so closely that our way of doing life is crowded out as his way flourishes within us.

Paul goes on to say, "All this is from God, who reconciled us to himself through Christ, and has given us the ministry of reconciliation" (2 Corinthians 5:18). Jesus is training us for this task. The central task of our new life in Christ is to share the love we have received. We are never fully reconciled to God until we are reconciled to our neighbor. Paul says that God gives us the ministry of reconciliation, such that

> in Christ God was reconciling the world to himself, not counting their trespasses against them, and entrusting the message of reconciliation to us. So we are ambassadors for Christ, since God is making his appeal through us; we entreat you on behalf of Christ, be reconciled to God.
>
> 2 Corinthians 5:19-20

Here Paul increases the level of expectation. We are Christ's ambassadors. The title of ambassador is a very specific honor. It denotes the trust of the ruler or country that confers this title. An ambassador represents the ruler or country and speaks for them in negotiations or other diplomatic assignments. As ambassadors, we are to exemplify the life, love, values, and grace of Jesus Christ everywhere we go. This means that you cannot look at race from the point of view of the family in which you were raised, the community where you grew up, or the culture in which you were immersed. You can't follow the preference of your undelivered, sinful, pre-Jesus heart.

In Christ you are a new creation. It may take some time to see people as clearly as Jesus saw them. Our goal is not to become "color-blind." I have a friend who is color-blind and it is not much fun. It makes it harder to understand what some traffic signs mean, and it can be a challenge to put clothes together that match. You don't want to be color-blind when you meet a person who is a native American and act like you don't know the history of their race in the United States for the past three hundred plus years. You don't want to treat the person from India like they are from Ghana or assume that all Caucasians are the same. Jesus doesn't make people color-blind or culture-blind or race-blind. Jesus can fill our hearts with love. When you combine love with intellect, you have both the motivation and the capacity to understand the context from which people come as well as the world in which they live.

This is the start of the work of racial reconciliation, which gives us the ability to be ambassadors for Christ who work to reconcile others to God. Such work is not possible when people sense that we believe that we are superior to them in some ways, or find them inferior in others. To be ambassadors, we must encounter others in the gracious way Jesus approached the woman at the well. We must allow Jesus to make us openhearted, so that we will see the great variety of human cultures and races as a source of beauty and strength. Jesus saw the world and its people this way because he was there when it was all lovingly created.

PEOPLE REALLY DO THIS

I emphasize that Jesus must make us a new creation for two reasons: we cannot do this on our own, and most of us think we were just fine before Jesus came into our lives. Rarely have I met anyone who thinks that they are prejudiced or racist toward others. I cannot speak for other races, but most white Americans I know who enter a conversation about racism spend the first several minutes with the observation that while they are sure the disease still exists, they are so glad not to be burdened with even the initial symptoms themselves. That is simply not the experience that people of other races have of us. Just about all of us have our own village in Samaria, where we would freak out if Jesus made us spend the night. We must address this, because when we hold bias or bigotry toward others, it compromises our ability to love others and be legitimate ambassadors for Christ in the world. The good news is that Jesus' love brings enormous credibility to our witness.

Robert Carter III found new life in Christ. He was transformed as a result. Robert was the grandson of Robert "King" Carter, one of the richest and most powerful men in the Virginia colonies. By the time of his death, King Carter had served as governor of Virginia and owned or controlled nearly three hundred thousand acres of land with farms and plantations.

When King Carter died, Robert Carter III received more than sixty-five thousand acres of land in Virginia and several hundred enslaved persons, who worked the land and generated a vast amount of wealth. About thirty years later, in 1777, Robert Carter III announced his conversion to Christianity after being influenced by a Baptist pastor. He believed that his salvation was through faith alone in Jesus Christ, and that he was a new creation because of his experience of God's love and mercy. Essentially, Carter believed that he had to live his life as Jesus would live if Jesus were him. In his time, abolitionists worked to end the practice of slavery. There were Methodist, Baptist, Presbyterian, and Quaker abolition movements, which grounded their arguments on the moral evil of slavery. They saw slavery as a great national sin that would have dire consequences in the future. With a righteous indignation reminiscent of biblical prophets, they called for its end and urged Americans to repent of it while there was time.[7]

In May 1782, the Virginia General Assembly passed "An act to authorize the manumission of slaves," which was a great victory for anti-slavery activists. Under this act, those who had title to enslaved people could legally offer them freedom. Robert Carter III saw this as an opportunity to do something monumental as a response to the lordship of Christ in his life. Beginning in 1791 he compiled a census of the slaves on his eighteen landholdings across five counties. He then executed a deed of emancipation for more than five hundred of his enslaved African Americans, gradually releasing them over several years. It is believed to be the largest emancipation of enslaved people by an individual in the United States.[8] Sadly none of Carter's children shared their father's belief about the evils of slavery, even though he intentionally had them educated in northern states where slavery was not practiced. His son George Carter fought the emancipation orders in court, especially those his father left in his will for an agent to enact after his death. While George's attempts to block emancipation were not successful, he brought enslaved people back to the farms he inherited from his father.

Carter's example shows us that when a person is deeply committed to Christ, he or she has to look at the life they are living and ask if the love of Christ is reflected in the way that I live, or if I simply hold the beliefs and practices of everyone else around me. Carter's friends, people like George Washington and Thomas Jefferson, did not understand him. His family was angered. Without enslaved people, they had no idea how to make profit off of their land. Emancipation cost him a great deal of money. Enslaved people had tremendous value and represented a sizable portion of the work force on his plantations as well as the economic capital that enabled him to borrow money and conduct business. Robert Carter III counted the cost and granted them freedom for one key reason: Jesus was his Lord. Carter took on the eyes of Christ and then made the personal changes he heard Jesus ask him to make.

Many washing machines still have an agitator to make clothes clean. At the base there are often four fins that push the clothes through the water. Spiritual practices are the fins Christ uses to stir up his love in our hearts. There are four practices that can be of great help in this area:

- Intentionality
- Vulnerability
- Confession
- Acts of Reconciliation

INTENTIONALITY

Start with intentionality. Over the past several years, I have intentionally read and studied both race in America and race issues in the state and town where I was raised in order to better understand the conflicted views I carry. It is easy to simply follow the prevailing practices and beliefs of those around us without question. Jesus asks more of us than this. It is essential that those of us who follow Christ examine what he is asking of us in our time.

This is especially true for someone like me, who has grown up and lives in a state where the majority of the population has gotten almost every important social issue of every generation wrong. Virginians supported slavery, offered to be the capital of the Confederacy, resisted Reconstruction, and overlooked the acts of terrorism of the Ku Klux Klan that included the lynching of black citizens, house burning, unlawful assembly, and general antagonism of all ethnic populations. In my state we did not want to give minority persons or women the right to vote. Jim Crow laws that limited constitutional rights for minority persons were upheld. Our politicians supported racial segregation of schools, transportation, and both public and private facilities even after the federal government said it was illegal.

When Richard and Mildred Loving, a white man and black woman, were married in Washington, D.C., in 1958, it was deemed illegal according to Virginia state law. Their house was stormed by the sheriff of their county at 2:00 a.m. They were charged with a felony under the "1924 Act to Preserve Racial Integrity" and sentenced to one year in prison. In lieu of this sentence, they promised the judge that they would not to return to Virginia together for twenty-five years. The Lovings had to take their case all the way to the Supreme Court, which ruled in their favor. The argument of Virginia's assistant attorney general Robert D. McIlwaine III, that the constitutionality of the state's law against interracial marriage was similar to regulations that prohibited incest and polygamy, was seen by the court to be as racist as it plainly was.[9]

I enjoy living in Virginia. However, I have come to realize that the list of things my state got completely wrong throughout history could fill several books of this size. This has been hard to face, because I was taught growing up that Virginians had a proud heritage, that leaders from our state, with just a little tiny bit of help from elsewhere, authored and created the greatest democracy in the world and won the Revolutionary War. I was told that we made major contributions to the vitality of the United States in every generation since. We were taught to take pride in our southern heritage.

Baby boomers were given textbooks that attempted to sanitize the past without any agitation. Facts were reinterpreted to create a more comfortable narrative. A seventh-grade textbook said that contact between English settlers and "Virginia's Indians" resulted in "a better life for both the settlers and the Indians." This seems odd since the descendants of the English settlers ended up owning all of the land while descendants of indigenous people were forced onto reservations. A high school textbook, *Cavalier Commonwealth*, showed an illustration of a well-dressed slave family arriving after a pleasant ocean voyage. The smiling new master shakes the hand of the father as his wife and four children, all in European hats and bonnets, eagerly wait their turn. According to this textbook, a slave "did not work so hard as the average free laborer, since he did not have to worry about losing his job."[10] This is the kind of thing I have been unlearning throughout my adult life.

You never know what you will find. While looking through a family genealogy, I read courthouse records with the names and dates for the Berlin side of my family back to the early 1700s. Included in the 1850 census of Winchester, Virginia, is the record of my ancestor, Jacob Mesmer. Under the names of his six children is a simple phrase, "9 slaves owned."

VULNERABILITY

That's it. No names. No birthdates. Nothing to record the existence of these children of God other than "9 slaves owned." I read about another relative who owned twenty-five enslaved people on his farm in Clarke County. It made me feel a little ill. It has been interesting to hear how others in my family experience this information. Some say that they experience no impact. They see it as something in the past that they did not choose and can neither control nor influence. "I'm not going to feel bad or guilty about something I didn't do" is one line of thought. But I resonate with my niece, who said, "Twenty-five slaves owned. That makes me sad. I feel bad about that. And I am fine with feeling bad about that."

While neither of us may need to feel bad, it is important that we allow ourselves to feel vulnerable to the ways those choices in our family impacted and benefited our lives. Consider the wealth those people generated for my family. Think about the capital that was passed down in our family, generation by generation, at the same time that these nameless enslaved people could not legally own or transfer any investments or wealth to their descendants. Think of the educations that it paid for, the money it generated, and the loans that were taken out on its good credit that advanced our economic future. No one has ever mentioned this in our family. One of those listed as owning slaves was my great-grandfather. For that not to be mentioned means that sometime after the Civil War, our people decided to either ignore or forget this part of our heritage.

It is obvious that I cannot undo the actions of my ancestors. But it has led to me to be vulnerable enough to realize that history is a part of my personal history. It makes me want to avoid what some authors call "white fragility." White fragility is the tendency white people often have to not talk about the injustice of the past or the prejudice and inequality of the present. White Christians must avoid such fragility, or we will never be able to receive the calling of God to work for justice in our time and agitate for change.

We must be willing to be vulnerable, just as the disciples had to be willing to feel vulnerable when they spent the night in the Samaritan town and undo all of that cultural training that was so ingrained into their hearts.

CONFESSION

If we can do that, then we can confess that we are not openhearted yet; but by the grace of God, we strive to grow in that direction. I want to confess something to you. There was a time, as an older child or teenager, when I told racial jokes, used the "n-word," verbally denigrated many racial groups and felt superior to people who did not look like me. I was overtly homophobic. If I was not misogynistic it was only due to the fact that my mother was a strong woman who would have none of that at any time. I was also raised in a community, nation, and culture that often taught me through overt lessons and subtle humor that people of color were inferior to white people.

The one environment I entered that seemed to affirm all people equally was the church. Sunday school teachers, pastors, and youth group leaders reinforced the message that we were all one in Christ Jesus. At the same time, the church was 99 percent middle class white people, and church was only a few hours a week. The tendency toward racism was not something that I confronted within myself until I was in college and seminary.

By learning the history of racial inequity, reading authors from a variety of backgrounds and countries, and most importantly, developing friends and colleagues who were different from me, I began to understand why it was important to not only acknowledge Jesus' call to love all people, but to actually allow Christ's lordship to transform my life in this way.

White people like me, who care about racial reconciliation, understand that even when the love and grace of Jesus transforms us, even when Christ motivates us to know and build relationships with people from other races and cultures, we may mess it up. We have some bad sectors on our hard drives. But it is worth the effort and risk of being intentional, vulnerable, and confessional so that we can move with others toward a reconciled space. This is necessary if we want to keep the Great Commandment and be ambassadors of the love of Christ that can transform human sin into loving relationships.

If we are being transformed, it will show in our commitment to both equality and justice for everyone, not just people who look and sound like us. That means that when you hear someone, especially a person who is not in the race of the majority population, speak of racism or injustice, you will start with a pause. Rather than lead with, "Well, those things may have been in the past, but I don't discriminate! I don't think that happens now," or "You just want me to feel guilty," just pause and listen. Take it in. If you have been intentional about understanding matters of race and culture and other places where people tend to be closed-hearted, you know if what is being said is consistent with what you have learned.

ACTS OF RECONCILIATION

A commitment to reconciliation means that you will ask Jesus what changes you need to personally make and what he wants you to do in your world. A good place to start is to stop doing things that do not come from a motivation of love or kindness. Racial jokes, stereotypes and words that minority groups find offensive can easily be removed from your conversation. If there are wrongs that you have committed, this is the time to apologize and, where appropriate, offer restitution. This is not about political correctness. It is about following the direction of the Holy Spirit and the willingness to submit to the lordship of Jesus Christ and God's command to love your neighbor. Consider where you can do good. It may be time to work on your relational circles and try to build relationships with people who are from a different culture or race with the hope of experiencing friendship and a deeper understanding of their context. Few things change people like real friendships with others. This is where we learn to care, gain a new perspective, show kindness, offer encouragement and support, and give and receive grace. Think on a larger plane as well, about a good you might join others in doing in your community. When you join community groups that are focused on justice and reconciliation, you will create opportunities for new relationships and be a part of the change that you want to see.

Openhearted living is often unpredictable. It is also never boring. Take a risk. Go to Samaria and spend a couple of days.

CHAPTER 5
VALUE THE VULNERABLE

I think I began learning that those who are happiest are those who do the most for others. This lesson I have tried to carry with me ever since.[1]

Booker T. Washington

Down the street from our church there is a 1920s era exhibition farm that is a part of the county park system. Frying Pan Park has barns and fields and is full of farm animals that people of all ages enjoy. Recently a new cow came to the farm. "Hokie," the twenty-month-old purebred Black Angus cow, was settling in nicely until the time came to clean her stall. She was kept in the barn by a 3.5-foot-tall wagon that blocked the entrance. Hokie decided to take a walk on the wild side. She measured the height of the wagon, thought, "I got this," and jumped over it, setting a new park record for the bovine vertical leap. Hokie hustled past shocked park employees, out the park entrance, and turned right on the aptly named West Ox Road. A half-mile later, she followed the flow of traffic past our church before veering right on the entrance ramp to Route 28 north, the eight-lane highway that connects to Dulles International Airport. One park employee followed by foot, another on an ATV, while others were in pursuit with a truck and trailer.

By this time police and firefighters were also hot on the hooves of the runaway cow. This was the first time they had been asked to pull over a twelve-hundred-pound charging heifer, and Hokie nimbly evaded their roadblocks. She continued north, toward the airport, possibly wondering if she would be late for her flight. Eventually she gave up and turned around. She crossed all four northbound lanes, jumped the jersey wall and rerouted down Route 28 south, all to the wonder of her fellow commuters. As she traveled the wrong way up an entrance ramp, a passing yet fascinated motorist got involved. He deftly pulled his vehicle alongside Hokie to corral her alongside another jersey wall until help arrived. A short time later, after a one-hour, two-and-a-half-mile pursuit, the runaway cow walked up the ramp into the park's cattle trailer. One employee said that Hokie looked very grateful for the ride that concluded her Angus adventure.

Jesus pursues people the same way the park employees chased that cow. His parable of the shepherd who leaves the ninety-nine sheep to find the one who wandered off is remarkably similar (Luke 15:3-7). Jesus does it with concern and determination. He understands the value of what is at stake when people jump the barriers and boundaries that protect them to find what seems like freedom. He cares when one of God's people is not enjoying the life for which they were intended. Many of us know what it is like to step on the welcome ramp God uses to bring us back into the fold. This sense of urgency to care for the vulnerable created a lot of conflict in his life.

Jesus meets a man in a synagogue who has a paralyzed hand. A group of Pharisees knows that Jesus can heal him, so they watch Jesus closely to see if he will do it on the Sabbath. They are hoping that he will, not in the hope that the man will regain the use of his hand, but so that they can bring Jesus up on charges for working on the Sabbath.

It was the same in social situations. A woman enters a dinner Jesus is attending at the home of a Pharisee and gratefully washes Jesus' feet with her tears and her hair. They are incredulous that Jesus is not showing this woman the door: "If this man were a prophet, he would have known who and what kind of woman this is who is touching him—that she is a sinner" (Luke 7:39).

The root of all that conflict is a simple question of who's in and who's out.

The Pharisees, scribes and Sadducees—the religious leaders of Judaism in Jesus' time—assumed that they were in. By in, I mean they felt that they lived within the will of God. They believed that they were in because they deserved to be in. They were fervent about keeping God's law. They studied and learned and sought to employ even the smallest strictures of the Mosaic law. And because they knew the law so well and outwardly fulfilled its requirements, they were impatient with people who did not. They became frustrated that others did not keep the law as they did. They judged others accordingly. This is a pitfall common among religious people that works against the Great Commandment to love God and neighbor. Those who are most committed, if they're not careful, can become self-righteous and begin to think that they should control the doors that determine who's in and who's out. It is especially true if you think that you are in, not because of God's love or God's grace, but because you have made the right decisions, done the right things and taken your commitments seriously, unlike those other people out there.

WHO'S IN, WHO'S OUT?

One of the easiest ways to make the commandment to love God and neighbor manageable is to identify large groups of people to whom this commandment does not apply. If we can reduce the number of people to whom the commandment to love applies, it gets much easier. Once we decide that some people are unworthy of our love or attention, we can safely place them far beyond the gravitational pull of our relational orbit. We no longer have to figure out how we will love them if we judge that they are not worthy of our love to begin with.

Think how much easier the love instruction now becomes to keep. There are far fewer people to love. Those who are still in bounds are probably much like me. If we get really good at saying who is out, we can whittle down considerably the number of people we believe God calls us to love. We don't need to condemn any of these persons, we can just tell ourselves that they are not worthy of our consideration. In this way we realize that the opposite of love may not be hate but unyielding neglect.

Jesus' love was free of categories and distinctions of who was more or less deserving. He lacked the ability to be unaware of, inattentive to, or judgmental of others. The content of these conflicts shows us a pattern of which groups of people the religious leaders assumed were out, and who Jesus knew was "in" the circle of God's love. It also shows us where Jesus was willing to sacrifice his reputation in order to heal or forgive someone. Observing Jesus, his disciples began to understand where they should place their priorities. When we are really dedicated to love, there are people we become willing to fight for, often the last people we would have ever thought we would make a priority. This is the remarkable thing about God's love. It takes you to people and places you would never choose to meet or go on your own.

That must be how the disciples felt as they stood near Jesus and spent time with people the Gospels collectively call "sinners." Often we are not even sure what specific sins they have committed. Based on the comments of the religious leaders who complained about Jesus, we know there were tax collectors, prostitutes, drunkards, and gluttons, among others. Rather than avoid these people, or fill his time and relational circles with the polished and refined, Jesus often interrupts his travel to have a meal with them, answer their questions, and even intervene when an angry mob wants to attack one. When Jesus met people who lived this way, he saw them not as bad people who needed to be judged but as lost people who need to be steered back to the God who loves them. He did not encourage poor morals or enable bad habits. Love is found in truth telling, difficult conversations, and boundary setting.

Another large group of people that received Jesus' attention were the "outcasts." This group would include people who were physically sick, emotionally ill and demon possessed, and those who struggled with chronic diseases like leprosy. When people became sick in his society, it was sometimes seen as a sign of God's curse. People with contagious diseases, like leprosy, were placed in groups apart from their families and villages and were forced to live at a distance from anyone. In a time when there was no framework to understand mental health or emotional illness, anyone who acted abnormally was assumed to be demon possessed. While I trust that evil is both present and powerful, I believe that some of those described in the Gospels as demon possessed may have suffered from the exact maladies that affect so many lives today. The woman today who pushes a shopping cart with her few possessions inside down the city street while muttering to herself in Jesus' time would have been considered demon possessed. The impact is the same, no matter how the condition is described. People tend to move away from such people, not toward them. Except Jesus. He encounters them not as people who are unsafe, but as people who are unseen.

Jesus also spent time with Gentiles, the non-Jewish people who lived in Israel. He healed a man at the request of a Roman centurion (Luke 7:1-10), and said that the man had great faith. Gentiles were immigrants to the country or members of the occupying army of the Roman Empire. Neither group was seen by the average person as a part of the people of God, yet Jesus healed them when asked (Mark 7:24-30) and praised them for their faith.

Finally, Jesus spoke good news to the poor. At that time, religious people often assumed that poverty was another sign of God's curse on your life. People did not think about whether your parents were literate or if you had access to education. Never mind whether you were born in a mansion or a shack. They simply assumed that if you were poor, it was a sign that you had sinned, and God was punishing you and withholding a blessing.

While the religious leaders often argued with Jesus about his interactions with people in these groups, he never failed to talk to them, attend to them, help and heal them. His disciples must have thought it was very odd when Jesus gave his time and energy to these people. A famous rabbi typically only mingled with the well, the wise, and the wealthy. Jesus spent his time with the least, the last, and the lost. The Pharisees, scribes, and Sadducees assumed such people were out and should not be considered for admission. They were happy to serve as gatekeepers, to keep people out and to let them feel both guilt and shame for their sin, scarcity, and sickness.

You may struggle with the same problem that I find difficult. I know Jesus has told me not to judge others, but I find it nearly impossible not to be judgmental of people who I think are being judgmental. Before anyone comes down too hard on these Jewish leaders, look over that list again and ask how much of your life is spent in a loving relationship with those found there. While we may not feel that people in such situations are cursed, we may not rush to get involved, even if these people are related to us. However, when we do get involved, when we care for the person who is sick by driving her to a doctor's appointment or visiting him in a rehabilitation center, we find that love gives a mutual blessing that renders the line between giver and receiver no longer visible. I have had people who are successful in business tell me that when they worked with an organization that helped a family move from homelessness to a secure place to live, it was more satisfying than any deal they had closed.

It is not easy to open yourself up to others, especially when the other person requires extra effort. I was in physical therapy one day. Across the room there was an older woman who walked with a limp. She was fully engaged, faithfully following the directions of the therapist. But she was moving slowly. It would be some time before she would walk at a normal pace. We shared a smile of encouragement with each other as we passed while moving between stations. She finished her session a few minutes before I did and left the clinic.

When I left, I could see her moving slowly down the long hallway to the elevator. She pressed the button, and I realized that I would have to wait for the elevator to return. Still at a distance, I kept walking toward the elevator. The doors began to close. Through the narrowing gap, I saw her look up and notice me in the hallway. Just as the door was about to close, her bony hand shot through the gap and grabbed one of the doors. Like some kind of elderly superhero in an Avengers movie, she pushed the door outward until it opened completely. She looked at me with a smile and said, "Would you like to join me and go down too?"

I want to be more like that. I would like to love other people enough to go to extraordinary measures to open the door and invite them in, rather than passively allow the door to close, go on my way and keep them out. Jesus said, "I am the gate.... All who came before me are thieves and bandits; but the sheep did not listen to them" (John 10:7).

Jesus encouraged his followers to become door openers rather than gatekeepers. He hoped that once people experienced the goodness of God, the love of God, and the grace of God, they would reside in it and be free to share it with others. This is why people who were sinners, outcasts, and poor loved Jesus and felt such joy in his presence. They were unaccustomed to being loved by someone who was talking about the ways of God. They knew that Jesus valued them, that he saw their worth, not one that they had earned or instilled within themselves. He saw their intrinsic value, the image of God that was imprinted upon their lives.

How does one become a door opener who leads others to the joy of Christ rather than a gatekeeper who judges others? Observing Jesus enables us to see how to value a vulnerable person. After Jesus stills the storm on the sea of Galilee, he and the disciples went across the lake to the region of the Gerasenes. They encountered a man who was said to have an unclean spirit. He was living among the tombs. This man was powerful, but he was also apparently angry and violent. No one could restrain him, even with chains. Mark describes his suffering in one sentence: "Night and day among the tombs and on the mountains he was always howling and bruising himself with stones" (Mark 5:5).

Mark wants us to notice that this man is out. At one time, he was probably in. He enjoyed a normal life in a beautiful Roman city. But now he lives amongst the dead in the cemetery. When he sees Jesus, he does something that is disconcerting. He begins to run toward Jesus. I picture the disciples, as they watch this out-of-control, strong man running toward them, grabbing the paddles and beginning to scamper back into the boat. If there was ever a time to avoid an outcast, this was it. But Jesus is going nowhere. He stands his ground. The man falls before Jesus and asks, "What have you to do with me, Jesus, Son of the Most High God?" (Mark 5:7).

JESUS REVEALS
WHAT OTHERS IGNORE

Something powerful happens in our faith when we attend to God's commandment to love others, especially those who do not have relationships, position, or wealth. Jesus is not about to ignore this man or act as though the power of God is not sufficient to help him out of his misery.

The first step Jesus took was to be intentional. I assume that the disciples thought this was a chance meeting. But it seems more likely that Jesus went to this side of the lake for this purpose. Undoubtedly people in the region talked about the distraught man who was forced to live in the cemetery. Jesus has made a divine appointment to see him. We wonder about the motivation. Few thought they could help him anymore. This man wasn't even Jewish, and he lived in a cemetery. It is clear that Jesus wanted his disciples to witness this encounter, an opportunity where Jesus reveals both the man's value and his vulnerability. When the man approaches, Jesus speaks to the unclean spirit in him and asks its name. "Legion," comes the reply, "for we are many" (Mark 5:9). This is a guy with a lot of issues. Jesus wants to know what they are. He wants the man to be healed.

Like the people in the villages near that cemetery, we often prefer to turn a blind eye to the demons in the lives of people we meet, or in our larger community, rather than make an effort to learn their names and evict them. It can feel like the demons are too big for us to handle. Families can avoid talk of someone's drug addiction for months before it becomes evident that there is a serious problem. A school down the street is negatively impacted by high crime rates in the streets that surround it, but no one shows up to ask how they might help the teachers succeed. Homeless people crowd the local shelter, but people in the community do not talk about the need for affordable housing, or ask city officials how that will be handled in the five-year plan. We put them out of sight and out of mind. While they may not get in our way, their presence tells us that the way of love is not being fully pursued.

JESUS DISRUPTS WHAT
HOLDS PEOPLE DOWN

Jesus casts all the bad stuff out of this man into a herd of swine who then run off a cliff. The pig herders tell the people of the nearby town and countryside. By the time they arrived, they found the formerly disturbed man sitting with Jesus, clothed and in his right mind. The disciples saw this kind of thing over and over with Jesus. Sickness was healed. Sanity was restored. Sins were forgiven. The broken were mended. People found new life. In person after person, the love of Christ disrupted what held people down.

We may not be miracle workers, but through this same love of Christ, we can work to disrupt what holds people down as well. I have friends whose daughter has struggled with a mental illness. She experiences depression and anxiety. First it was mild, but as the years went on, it became more severe. She dropped out of college and came home. She feared leaving her house. Then she did not want to leave her room. She continued to withdraw from her life and the people who gave it meaning. Her parents worried and felt helpless, but their love was fierce. They prayed for her. They were patient. They became persistent. They encouraged her. They found her a counselor. They worked with a doctor. Weeks turned into months, but they did not give up their faith in God, their love of their child, or the hope that health could return. One day I looked at my Facebook stream and realized a miracle had occurred. Here is what their daughter posted:

> I am finally ready to come out and tell everyone what's been going on with my life.
>
> Some of you may know this, but I've been dealing with depression and anxiety on and off for many years now. My work and schooling have been affected by this. I have not been able to keep a stable job or been able to go to and pass classes because of it. I have a mental illness called agoraphobia, which is the fear of being in social situations or being in places that I don't feel comfortable in. For the past 2 months I have not been able to leave the house at all. I was starting to become hopeless. However, for the

past few months my parents and I have been looking into residential programs that help people with mental illness get better. We have finally been able to find one. I want to say sorry to all my friends that I haven't been in contact with this year because of everything that's been going on. I miss you and I feel that I have lost some friends along the way because of this. I have seen your texts and listened to your voicemails. I miss you all so much, but I didn't know how to talk to people with everything I've been dealing with.

As pleased as I was to read the honesty of her post, I was also encouraged by the responses she received. Friends wrote to encourage her. People she thought had given up on her began to make contact. People she did not know cared for her expressed their encouragement. She discovered that she was valued. Her vulnerability was a source of inspiration to others who also suffer from depression, anxiety, or other forms of mental illness. Her willingness to partner with others for support in her healing disrupted the power of her mental illness just enough to take the next steps in the process. Not only were people at work to disrupt what held her down, with her courageous post, she had the courage to disrupt what also held others down. As she communicated the truth of her life, she blessed lives in her various relational circles.

JESUS REDEEMS WHAT OTHER PEOPLE FORSAKE

The Gerasene man wanted to go with Jesus. I assume that he was motivated by gratitude. I am sure that after having been so ill, he wanted to be near the one who had restored him. He begged Jesus to let him get in the boat and follow him. Instead, Jesus gave him something to do. He entrusted him with a mission.

"Go home to your friends, and tell them how much the
Lord has done for you, and what mercy he has shown
you." And he went away and began to proclaim in the
Decapolis how much Jesus had done for him; and everyone was amazed.

Mark 5:19-20

Jesus does not bring this man back to Israel. The reason could be that few would listen to a Gentile talk about God's power and consideration for their life. Instead, Jesus sends the man home, back to his family and friends, to share how much God loves him. He goes to his own community, to the people who knew he was not in his right mind. He tells them that there is hope for those who stand in the light of Christ's love. Now there is a new story being shared. No longer is it the story of the guy who was so sick that he was forced to live in the cemetery so that no one would get hurt. Now there is the story of the man whose life has been saved by Jesus. It is a story of God's power; but it is also a story of the love of Christ, who did not run when the man approached him and was willing to heal him even though they did not share the same culture or religion. Now the man has the opportunity to offer hope to others, to tell them what God could do in their lives. It's not a hard message to share. They already believe that if God can help this man, he can help anyone.

Jesus wants to bless you and he wants you to have the joy of blessing others. It's not enough for him that you would be healed. He wants to put the power in your life that could help heal someone else so that your joy will increase beyond measure. The critical power that Jesus can offer us is the ability to love others because we see the value not only of who they are, but who, with God's help, they can be. Don't worry if you don't feel valuable right now. Jesus knows something important about your future. The history and damage of your past, the stuff we hope to disguise, ignore, and never disclose, is exactly what is most likely going to enable you to bless others somewhere down the road.

HOW DO WE LOVE
THE VULNERABLE?

Be Curious

I am not a tattoo person. I am not against what others do, but I am committed to avoiding needles and decisions that are permanent enough to require lasers to remove. That is how I think about tattoos now. Years ago, however, I was judgmental of others' decisions, especially in the years before tattoos went mainstream and everybody had one. The Holy Spirit told me that I was condemning and suggested I stop it. But I didn't. Then one day I decided that rather than be judgmental about the tattoo, I could be interested in the person under the tattoo. I didn't know exactly how to do that, so I took some risks.

I started asking strangers to tell me the stories of their tattoos. I asked people on hotel shuttles and in airplanes. I talked to servers in restaurants. I asked on the beach (you have to be really careful when you ask on the beach). I discovered that almost everyone will tell you their tattoo story. I found the stories fascinating and came to appreciate that almost every tattoo has a story behind it. The stories were so compelling that I decided to start a tattoo website with a friend. I had cards printed with the site on them. I would hand them out and ask people to put the story of their tattoo on the website.

It was a terribly unsuccessful website, because so few people actually wrote up their story, but it cured me of being judgmental and I met a lot of very nice people, which seemed worth the two hundred dollars I spent on the website and cards. And I think that the Holy Spirit got a kick out of it. My kids were always embarrassed when I asked people about their tattoos, but I found curiosity a much more loving posture than judgment. I also came to understand that when I am curious about someone, they often feel valued. It is easy to care about people after you know their story and hard to judge them.

I think that is what Jesus had in mind for us. Knowing people's stories ignites the caring God desires for us to extend. An easy way to love others is to start with a question. Listen to their story. Don't rush in with solutions or advice or offer up your latest big idea. Be inquisitive and attend to what people offer you. Rome was not built in a day and trust is not built in a minute.

When the church I serve partnered with The United Methodist Church in Sierra Leone, Africa, to help children avoid child labor and care for the sick with a small hospital, I attended a lot of meetings with our African partners. During those meetings I had many things I wanted to say. I learned that I often did not know what I was talking about because I had not asked enough questions to understand the culture and the context in which we were trying to do good. I tried to become more curious, listen carefully, and hear the wisdom of the people in the room who actually resided on the continent where our projects were located. I found that over time, when people know you are curious about them, and will hear them when they offer something, you can build deep and abiding friend-ships with them. Trust is built when people feel valued. Then, when you have something to offer, they are twice as likely to consider the ideas that you share.

Engage

Since my friend Tim retired, he has made valuing the vulnerable a part-time job. Tim decided that he didn't just want to think about the prob-lem of homelessness, he wanted to do something. He started working with an organization near his home. He brought best practices to churches who wanted to be a part of the effort. He got to know people who are homeless in his community by name. He spent time talking to them. He heard their stories. He offered help where he could, and he learned a lot about the reasons that these people live on the streets. He is especially motivated in the winter, and worries, not about "the homeless," but about Frank and Jimmy, Lou Ann and Tony.

Tim met one man who brought him particular concern. When Tim talked to Manuel, he seemed disoriented. Over time he realized that the source of Manuel's confusion was not drugs or alcohol, which he first suspected, but the onset of dementia. It would be easy to walk away at that point. It is very difficult to find ongoing care for a man who has very little income and who does not want to enter a facility of any sort. Tim did some digging. He asked around about Manuel. He talked to people and learned that Manuel had come from Mexico. At one time he was a very fine artist. He was successful. He also had family members back in Mexico. Sometime earlier, Manuel started to change. He gave up his work. He made bad financial decisions. He ended up on the street. Tim was working with a pastor in the community to help Manuel. Together they found Manuel's brother in Mexico. Tim connected with Manuel's family through Facebook, and eventually spoke with Manuel's niece.

It turns out that the family was very interested in Manuel's welfare, but no longer knew how to contact him. He had stopped calling years earlier and they had no way to reach him. They feared that he was dead. Tim began working with the pastor and Manuel's family. He and the pastor got Manuel a plane ticket from the Mexican Embassy. Tim asked our church to pay for the pastor's plane ticket so that he could accompany Manuel to make sure that he got to his family in Mexico safely. When they landed, the family was happy to have Manuel back in their lives. Tim and the pastor were happy to have Manuel off the street. But all I could think about was that it only happened because my friend Tim decided to learn the name of the homeless man who spent all his time living in the woods and wandering the streets in a town nearby.

If you want to love people, especially vulnerable people, you will have to take the risk of engaging people and situations that are different from what you know and unexpected for someone like you. The disciples followed Jesus and heard him say that they would be blessed if they would care for the sick or feed the hungry. Then they saw him do these things. He touched the leper. He fed the crowds. He stopped to hear the woman talk about her uncontrolled bleeding. They saw that Jesus was engaged, and they realized they would have to be too if they wanted to become like their rabbi.

Have Expectations

The white-water rafting guide was nice but firm as we started down the river. We would go through class II-V rapids. We would need to work together and we would need to focus on what we were doing to have an enjoyable day. We had signed enough release forms in the outfitters office to make me think that someone was convinced I might die. We practiced a few maneuvers and followed his commands, turning the big raft left and right or spinning it around. Then he gave us what he called "The Rules of the River."

Rule One: "Don't fall out of the raft unless you are told to do so."

This is an important rule because the guide's job is to get the raft down the river and through the rapids. These rapids can be dangerous, more so if you are floating through them by yourself with the aid of your life jacket instead of inside a giant rubber raft with your friends.

Rule Two: "If you fall out, you must be an active participant in your own rescue."

The guide was very clear with us, "This is not a cruise ship. If you fall out, don't just float helplessly. Make your way toward the raft. We will throw you a line. Hold on to the line firmly. Do not drop the line. Once you get near the raft, don't become dead weight. We will grab you and help you on board, but you must put out your arms and use your legs to get onto the raft so that we can quickly focus ourselves on the rapids again."

I remember the speech very well because it occurred to me that it might be good information to have downstream. "You must be an active participant in your own rescue" is not just a good rule for the river. It is a good rule for life. We know or come across people who are vulnerable because they hit some rapids and fell out of their raft. A company is sold, a department is downsized, or an evaluation turns up poor performance and they pop out of the employment raft. A medical exam comes back with bad results and we are thrown from the health raft. A couple grows distant, spouses grow irritable, angry, and rude, and soon they have slipped from the relationship raft. An addiction makes it hard to work and hard to cope and soon someone has fallen from the functional life raft.

It is appropriate to have expectations, even for hurting, vulnerable people. Jesus had expectations of his disciples. He had expectations for people he healed and forgave. He asked one man if he really wanted to be healed, because it looked like he had come to enjoy lying by the pool of Beth-zatha (or Bethsaida) (John 5:6). He told people what they needed to do, or not do, as the case may be, once he forgave them and where they should go after he healed them.

Jesus calls us to reach out to people in troubled water. We have the ability to help. We can throw a line and work to hoist them onto the raft, but we can't help people who do not realize they must be an active participant in their own rescue. With a few notable exceptions, like children who are too young or elderly people who are too frail, you cannot do for others what they will not do for themselves. When you try to figure out how to help a vulnerable person and you have identified an appropriate way to do so, it is important to listen to their response. You may hear something like this:

"That is just the way I am. I can't help it."

"The problem is not with me, it is with my boss's unrealistic expectations."

"Doctor, I don't like to exercise, and I'm not big on following directions."

"I am not addicted. I have it under control."

"You have to understand that when I get angry, I scream a lot. I can't help it."

This is the equivalent of a former raft member floating in the water while calling out, "I'm fine," "It's not that bad," or "I think you are overstating the power of those rapids up ahead."

Christ's love enables us to be patient with others, but it is important to remember we only have power to change ourselves. We have influence that can encourage and support change in others. We can consistently walk beside, be present, and communicate what we are willing to do, but the next faithful step people take in their healing is their own.

Be Kind

The best way to start being kind is to avoid being mean.

Monika Allen was excited when *Self* magazine contacted her and asked if they could use a picture of her and a friend running the New York City marathon. Monika ran the marathon wearing a tutu while dressed as Wonder Woman. Her friend was Supergirl, also in a tutu. The writer at *Self* ran the picture in its "BS" section, calling the tutu "lame" and adding "now if you told us they made people run away from you faster, maybe we would believe it."[2]

Allen was shocked that her photo was used this way. She went to the magazine's Facebook page and explained that she was wearing the Wonder Woman costume because it was how she felt about herself that day. This was the first marathon she had run since the discovery of her inoperable brain tumor. She was able to run even though she was in the middle of a course of chemotherapy. The tutu, Allen explained, was not for speed, but fundraising. She made and sold them to financially support "Girls on the Run," a program that promotes better health for girls.

It was a bad day to be *Self* magazine as friends of Monika and later many, many others who became aware of this story shared their thoughts on Facebook and Twitter. Editor-in-chief Lucy Danziger later wrote, "On behalf of Self, we sincerely apologize for our inadvertent insensitivity. I have personally reached out to Monika and her supporters online to apologize for the misstep and tell them we are trying to remedy the situation. At Self we support women such as Monika; she is an inspiration and embodies the qualities we admire. We have donated to her charity and have offered to cover her good work in a future issue. We wish her all the best on her road to good health."[3]

It was good that the editor-in-chief apologized. But how was that snarky caption considered a good idea in the first place? It happened because the writer only saw a silly costume that included a tutu and took a jab. They made a judgment about Monika and her friend. When they called to seek permission to run the photo, they failed to ask Monika why she wore the tutu and the costume. The writer was creating an inside joke. "Hey readers, we're in, she's out. They are less. We are more."

My goal is not to demonize the person who placed the caption under Monika Allen's picture or *Self* magazine. Many of us have committed the same kind of "inadvertent insensitivity" the editor spoke of in her apology in order to produce a quick laugh or moment of camaraderie with friends. Moments when we are unloving do not require negative emotions like anger or revenge. They often happen in the normal course of our work and life. This is why it is so important to have the rule of Christ's love in your life that leads to acts of kindness and makes words and actions of contempt or cruelty feel unnatural and out of place, like you put a slice of orange in your mouth only to discover it was a lemon. Love must be a rule for us, or we will never become consistent in the commandment to love the Lord our God with all our heart, with all our soul, and with all our might.

It is remarkable what kindness does for us and others. I was in a physical therapy office recently and was invited to write down some information on a piece of paper. I was told I could use a pen from a nearby work station. When I picked it up, I saw a note that the person had taped to her desk lamp. Underneath a small heart, in a child's handwriting, it read, "Thank you for helping people."

I have wondered about that note for some time since I saw it. It is possible that it came from a child whom this person helped in the course of her work. It could be a note from her child, after hearing what she did during the workday. It was so meaningful to the occupant of that space that she placed it where she would see it daily, perhaps as a reminder to herself, or maybe just to recall the kindness of the child who offered it. That note had such impact that it made me want to do what it described. One heart. Five words. Never underestimate the power of the smallest act of kindness that you offer others.

CHAPTER 6
EMULATE CHRIST

If you could only sense how important you are to the lives of those you meet; how important you can be to the people you may never even dream of. There is something of yourself that you leave at every meeting with another person.[1]

Fred Rogers

A friend was telling me about her grandson's day at preschool. When he came to her house, he was very excited and said it was a great day because in the morning, a firefighter came to tell them about firetrucks and ambulances. He was very excited to see the firefighter's helmet, burn-proof coat, boots and other equipment.

"Then during chapel time, we heard a story about Moses."

"Which one?" his grandmother asked.

"The one about the burning bush," he replied.

"What did you think about the story?" she asked.

"I think that Moses should have called 911," he replied.

I wonder if Moses ever looked back on the moment that God called him to lead the people of Israel, and thought the same thing.

Throughout the Bible, God calls people to do difficult things. Keeping the Great Commandment to love God fully and to love your neighbor as yourself may be one of the most difficult. While our innate tendencies to self-centered actions and responses are a part of the complexity, another part of our difficulty is found in the remarkable example of love expressed in Jesus' life that we are called to follow. Jesus shows us the hands and heart of love. When you read the Gospels and picture Jesus as he lived and carried out his ministry, you can see his hands at work. He offers a hand up for the paralyzed man healed by his touch. He puts a hand out to the woman caught in adultery and puts her on her feet with an experience of mercy and new life based on her future decisions rather than her past mistakes. Jesus' expressive hands move when he shares his wisdom with a crowd about life with God through a parable.

He lends a hand with his disciples to pass out bread as they feed the five thousand. Jesus places a gentle hand on the shoulder of a mourning father as he weeps over the death of his daughter before Jesus extends his healing hand to revive her. Jesus gets his hands dirty when he washes his disciples' feet. He is even-handed as he shares the first Communion with them, serving Judas as well as the other eleven. In the garden of Gethsemane, we see Jesus' hands folded in prayer, as he again experiences a quiet and deep communion, the oneness with the Holy Trinity that has directed his life. His hands are wounded as he is nailed to a cross, an event that he willingly endured for the redemption of the world. When Jesus showed his pierced hands to the disciples to prove that the resurrected body they saw was the same as the one crucified and not a figment of their imagination, they were looking at the perfect symbol of his love.

THE PROBLEM OF CONSISTENCY

Interestingly, we cannot have Jesus' hands without Jesus' heart, and we probably won't cultivate Jesus' heart until our hands are accustomed to working in the ways of Christ. In order to love the Lord our God with all our heart, soul, mind, and strength and love our neighbor as ourselves, there must be a correlation between our hands and our heart. Jesus has given us quite a standard to follow. High standards are difficult, yet possible, when we make them our pursuit.

I remember when it was announced that Baltimore Orioles shortstop Cal Ripken, Jr. had broken Lou Gehrig's record for the most consecutive baseball games played. The "Iron Man" had crossed the 2,131-game mark. Before his retirement, Ripken would play 2,632 consecutive games over more than sixteen years without a break related to injury, vacation, or time off for good behavior. Ripken set a new standard in his sport for consistency of play and lack of injury. He raised the bar more than a few notches. Some argue that Ripken's record will never be broken. To give you an idea about how high the standard has been raised, at the time of this writing, the current player with the highest number of consecutive games played is held by Kansas City Royals shortstop Alcides Escobar. Escobar is an elite athlete with remarkable skills. Any baseball player would find his recent streak admirable. However, it ended at 421 sequential games played.[2] As good as it is, it does not even break the top thirty of the list that Ripken leads. Now he is back to zero. Ripken has set a truly remarkable standard in his game.

Jesus gave his disciples a new standard for love when he said, "I give you a new commandment, that you love one another. Just as I have loved you, you also should love one another. By this everyone will know that you are my disciples, if you have love for one another" (John 13:34-35).

When I hear Jesus speak that commandment, I feel like I just walked onto a baseball diamond with guys like Cal Ripken, Jr., Lou Gehrig, and Alcides Escobar. In my current state, I am not going to make the cut. I wouldn't be allowed to be a batboy during team practice. When it comes to your desire to love others consistently, if you ever felt like you are not making the standard, you are in good company. If you have ever been called a hypocrite or told that you were a phony or a fraud by someone who knows you, or by your inner voice, it may be the distance between the utter consistency of Jesus' head and heart and the number of broken streaks in ours. High standards provide both aspiration and inspiration. They help us understand the greater goal for which we stretch ourselves.

A NEW STANDARD

Many good people, many dedicated Christians, are saddened by their inability to keep Jesus' commandment to love others as he loved us. Never give up on yourself, and remember that the first disciples had the same problem. The Gospel of John has what many consider to be the most intense portrayal of the last week of Jesus' life. The author tells us that Jesus used this time with great intentionality because he knew that "the Father had given all things into his hands, and that he had come from God and was going to God" (John 13:3).

Here the nature of Jesus' journey with his disciples will fundamentally change. The disciples have followed Jesus for about three years at this point. The time of Jesus' crucifixion and death is near. Before he leaves his disciples, he gives them some final instruction in the new standard of love he expects from them. They are to love one another as he has loved them. It is hard to be optimistic about their odds of success when their journey will be their own. While Jesus teaches about humility, they argue over who is the greatest disciple. When he demonstrates servanthood, they argue over who will get the best seat at the table.

When we read this new commandment to love each other as Jesus loves us, we must remind ourselves that Jesus is not encouraging them to singular acts of kindness. He is not suggesting that they become nicer to their elders or kinder to their pets. He is saying that their whole testimony depends on whether they love others as he loved them. Jesus wants us to understand that people will know that we are his disciples by our love. Jesus has issued us both a great challenge and a kind invitation.

WAKE RESPONSIBILITY

Years ago, I was with a friend who was taking his boat from Virginia to North Carolina on the Intracoastal Waterway. I had never traveled by boat before and enjoyed the smooth ride and the opportunity to see the rivers and inlets that fed into the watercourse. I soon realized that there was a community of boats, some of which traveled seasonally from Boston, Massachusetts, all the way to southern Florida. We passed the massive cruise ships docked in the shipbuilding yards of Norfolk, Virginia. There were Navy ships, tugs, barges, private craft, and a variety of commercial fishing boats. Because of the varying sizes of boats and ships that use the waterway, you have to pay attention to the speed you travel. The wake of larger ships and boats can be disastrous to the smaller watercraft that use the same route, which is rather confined in many places. That message was made plain when we pulled into a marina at the end of our first day. Signs attached to poles in the channel warned boats to slow down as they approached the harbor entrance. They stated that the wake from the boat could damage other craft that were tied up at the marina. The final warning sign before the marina stated in large, bold, capital letters: "YOU ARE RESPONSIBLE FOR YOUR OWN WAKE."

As a pastor, I have met with a lot of people who did not understand that they are responsible for their own wake. I know what it is like to forget that principle myself. Some come with stories of how others have hurt them. Others share regrets for missed opportunities to show love to others or times when they were angry or even hateful to someone. It is often someone they knew well, a family member or colleague at work. Their wake knocked another person over or damaged a number of people just as the wake of a speeding craft coming into the marina would slam all the boats in its path onto the pilings to which they were tied.

Respectful boat captains are mindful of others on the water and understand what is sometimes called "wake responsibility." They think about the distance of their boat from the shore, a dock, or other watercraft. They keep their music down and their eyes alert to others. They notice their speed and slow it down when it serves others. Much of wake responsibility is about avoiding harm to the people around you. Wake management in our lives requires loving neighbor as self with a consistent and conscious effort to avoid harming others at all costs.

However, following the example of Christ goes beyond simply avoiding harm. It also produces good things. Think of what would happen if you lavished love on the people around you. In your wake, others would experience thoughtful, even gentle words instead of the slicing speech or cold shoulder that they anticipated from you. Your wake of love would leave some people with the experience of forgiveness. Others, expecting you to judge them for their appearance, dress, or lifestyle would feel better about themselves after you shared your kind comments or words of encouragement. They would have a greater desire be kind to others because of their experience with you. Jesus invites us to manage our wake for the duration of the journey. His commandment to love takes us way beyond disconnected moments of kind events or intermittent politeness. Here we are told to love other people the way Christ loved them.

I don't think we can do this on our own. A time or two, yes. A two-week streak, possibly. It is the season after season, year after year part of this call that is so difficult. Often people work up to love on an as-needed basis. Most can be loving, forgiving, patient, or compassionate during critical periods of life. Love as a strategy for a portion of the journey, compared to love as a way of being throughout the journey, are two different experiences. The question we ask is how to show up on this field day after day to keep love in play in both good seasons and bad.

SERVANTHOOD

To stay in step in upholding this commandment, we must emulate Christ. To emulate is to imitate in such a way as to form a practice or habit. It is to take on the ability of the one from whom you learn. We must live and love like Jesus. To emulate Christ requires the love of Jesus to be so firmly embedded in our hearts that it is expressed in the words and actions of our lives. Our eyes must be so firmly fixed on Jesus that he enables us to see and love others as he loved them.

It was only in retrospect that the disciples truly understood what Jesus was showing them a few days before his death. When Jesus shared his new commandment to love as he loved, it was during a Passover meal with his disciples. He set the stage for that moment at the beginning of that meal. Before anything else happened, he stood up, took a towel and a basin of water and one by one, washed their feet. This made no sense to the disciples. No rabbi stoops down and washes the feet of his followers. With the exception of podiatrists and a few others who make, repair or sell shoes, the rule is easily observed: the more respected you are, the higher you go, the further away you get from people's feet.

Most people I know have never experienced foot washing in the context of a dinner invitation. Covered by shoes, our feet do not attract the dust and grime that people in Jesus' day experienced. The communication power of this servant-oriented act may be lost as a result. We can still easily understand the discomfort the disciples displayed. If you want to get a sense of this, gather a group of your friends for dinner. Before the meal begins, take out a basin, some water, and a towel, and tell them that you would like to wash their feet. I predict that a comfortable room of old friends, whose easy-going and relaxed conversation fills the air, will suddenly become as tense and strained as the head of a drum. The reasons are many:

"I am not ready for this."

"You don't want to see them."

"No one touches my feet but me."

"That is a bit too familiar for me."

Such an offer will drive out new communication skills in the person most prone to conflict avoidance. There will be a few who might accept. They probably have experience with professionals who provide pedicures. Even they may refuse your offer. Without proper payment, they do not want to see you take on the role of a servant to those who are perfectly able to wash their own feet.

This concern for roles and position was present in Jesus' day. In that time, a good host would provide water and a towel and let you wash your feet. A wealthy host would have a servant wash your feet. Jesus is the only host who would become a servant and wash the feet of his followers. Their discomfort occurs when he crosses a line of what a rabbi would acceptably do for his disciples.

There is a reason that this scene of Christ stooping down to wash the feet of his followers is iconic not only to Christians, but to anyone who has heard about Jesus' life and teaching. For the disciples, it was a poignant moment of experiential learning that would inform their understanding of Jesus' commandment to love others. The author of the Gospel of John knew that. He opens this setting by telling us, "Jesus knew that his hour had come to depart from this world and go to the Father. Having loved his own who were in the world, he loved them to the end" (John 13:1).

"To the end" speaks of both the quality and duration of Jesus' love. The narrator tells us that that in this act of love and grace, Jesus uses his hands to communicate his love in an act of humble servanthood. Jesus loved them "to the fullest." When he completes this task and is seated at the table, Jesus then says,

> "So if I, your Lord and Teacher, have washed your feet,
> you also ought to wash one another's feet. For I have set
> you an example, that you also should do as I have done

> to you. Very truly, I tell you, servants are not greater than
> their master, nor are messengers greater than the one
> who sent them. If you know these things, you are blessed
> if you do them.
>
> John 13:14-17

Our calling as Christ-followers is to be servants to the people we love. To those we don't know, we are called to live out of a guiding ethic of love that enables us to know what to do in the moment. Rather than carry a list of rules that would anticipate the situations that may appear on our journey, we simply do what Christ's rule of love directs us to do. Opportunities are all around us.

Hunter Shamatt realized his wallet was missing not long after he arrived for his sister's wedding. He was anxious about how he would make the return trip without his identification, and how he would make his school loan and vehicle payments without the four-hundred-dollar paycheck and sixty dollars that were inside. He assumed that he lost it on the flight he took from Omaha to Las Vegas. He called the airline, but no one had seen it. When the weekend was over, after a lengthy interview in the airport, he was able to travel home. The next day, a package arrived at his home with his name on it. Inside was his wallet with a note:

"Hunter, found this on a Frontier flight from Omaha to Denver—row 12, seat F wedged between the seat and wall. Thought you might want it back. All the best." The note was signed, "TB."

Hunter noticed that the contents of his wallet were not the same as when he last saw it. Everything was there—the check, his license and his cash—but was the victim of reckless rounding. The good news was that the stranger rounded up and shared the reason at the end of the note:

"P.S. I rounded your cash up to an even $100 so you could celebrate getting your wallet back. Have Fun!!!"

Hunter was so shocked that he counted the money three times.

"No way, no way," Hunter remembers saying. "That can't be. No way, just no way."

Hunter's family wanted to thank this thoughtful person. His mother posted a picture of the note on social media. Hundreds and then thousands of people liked and shared the picture of the note. Eventually, someone who worked with Todd Brown identified him based on some things he had shared and helped the Shamatts connect to him.

Hunter wrote Todd a note of appreciation:

> "Sir, I can't thank you enough. What you've done for me is virtually unheard of. Never in my life have I or my family witnessed such generosity. I never expected to see my wallet again, let alone with $40 more. Thank you so much, I've got student loans and a truck loan, and it makes all the difference."[3]

Forty dollars is not exactly the most generous gift I have ever heard of, but it is a remarkable act of love. It is meaningful not in its amount, but in its degree of thoughtfulness. Here we see someone who leaves a wake of good things as he goes through the journey of life. To return the wallet would have been more than enough. To add forty dollars as a way to encourage the recipient is what could be described as godly, in that it emulates the many moments of Jesus' unexpected generosity to us.

John Wesley, the Anglican priest who started the Methodist movement, helps us understand the importance of serving our neighbor as an opportunity that comes from God and flows to God. He admonished the early Methodists to understand that it was through their service of others that they served God, and in so doing, expressed their love to God. Wesley wrote, "One of the principal rules of religion is, to lose no occasion of serving God. And, since he is invisible to our eyes, we are to serve him in our neighbour; which he receives as if done to himself in person, standing visibly before us."[4]

Wesley understood the point Jesus made in another fundamental text related to servanthood found in the Gospel of Matthew. In the parable of the great judgment, those who are found to have pleased the king are those who served him. They served the king food when they observed hunger, offered water to quench thirst, showed hospitality when the king was a stranger, gave clothing when needed, offered care when the king was sick, and even visited the king in prison. The only problem is that the righteous people to whom the king attributes all of these actions have no memory of serving him this way. They are happy the king is pleased, but they have no idea what he is talking about. Jesus shares the critical lesson of this story when he says that the king answered them, "Truly I tell you, just as you did it to one of the least of these who are members of my family, you did it to me" (Matthew 25:40).

There is a reason that sentence is so memorable to us that it has motivated millions of acts of kindness, generosity, and love since the time Jesus shared it. When we take on the posture of servanthood and begin to care for those around us as much as we care for ourselves, we live into the balance of life found in the Great Commandment that calls us to love God, our neighbor, and ourselves. There is a unity of love that Jesus calls his disciples to seek through the commandment and his teaching on love throughout the Gospel. This call to love all people, and through this means express our love of God, is a unique tenet of the Christian faith. During a recent lecture, Dr. Sathi Clarke of Wesley Theological Seminary observed this dynamic when he said, "The uniqueness of the Christian gospel is the fact that what is offered by Jesus Christ is that you cannot have only God alone and you cannot only have brother and sister alone. Becoming whole for the purposes of God involves both loving God and loving each other."

SACRIFICE

While Jesus afforded his disciples the training to emulate his way of living though three years of daily life together, he knew that before they would ever complete their journey of love, he would have to take a journey of his own, without them. It must have been odd when Jesus began to talk about his death on a cross. They could not imagine him going anywhere without them. After all the hours they had shared and all the instructions they had followed, they did not believe that they would not be willing or able to follow a path that Jesus took. But Jesus knew that the cross would be a solitary experience. Every cross is. He told his disciples, in the year prior to his arrest, that he would die, and that his death would take place on a cross. His disciples were adamant in their denial of this prediction of a criminal's punishment. This sounded both unbelievable and reckless. In the minds of the disciples, this prediction either could not happen, or should be avoided at all costs. They wanted to believe that he would continue their journey indefinitely.

We should not be surprised that Jesus' disciples were in denial. Most of us live life trying to avoid death—and even conversation about death. Ask any attorney about the preparation of a will and you will understand. Karen and I once made time with an attorney to draw up a will. The work was done, and we received a call to set up a time to review and sign the documents. Suddenly we could find no time for this twenty-minute appointment. We put it off, set a date, and then rescheduled going by the office. Twice. I apologized to the office manager and she said, "Don't worry about it. People do this all the time. It's probably not really about your schedule. Nobody wants to sign their own will."

Jesus, however, spoke of his death, predicted his death, and even embraced his death. His final journey is called the "Via Dolorosa" or the way of suffering. When Jesus walked the path to Golgotha, the hill on which he was crucified, it was neither a barren track nor a lonely path, as artists sometimes portray. Jesus carried his cross through city streets, past customers in the market and past alleys where shopkeepers put up displays of their goods. The intentionality of Jesus' sacrifice was on full display. John tells us that he carried his own cross. This Gospel account is void of stumbling. There is no dropping the cross. There is no Simon of Cyrene to take on the burden of its weight the final distance up the hill.

Jesus walks alone to make a gift of love. He does this with great purpose. On more than one occasion Jesus had told his disciples that he would take this journey, so that they would pay attention and understand what he was going to accomplish on the cross. His last words before death are, "It is finished" (John 19:30). Here he speaks not of the end of his life, but the accomplishment of his mission. He knows that he has been light in a dark world. He has been the bread of life for those who hunger for God. He has been the Good Shepherd, and now he lays down his life for the sheep.

Jesus lays down his life for those he loves, and it includes all the world. In his crucifixion he shows us a love that will go the distance and offer everything. With Jesus, there is no holding back or resistance to sacrifice. There is no consideration of what's best for him. The cross is a powerful symbol because it reminds us of the unequivocal love of God, and the offer of hope and life. The Gospel of Matthew records Jesus' clear understanding of the purpose of his death, "He took a cup, and after giving thanks he gave it to them, saying, 'Drink from it, all of you; for this is my blood of the covenant, which is poured out for many for the forgiveness of sins'" (Matthew 26:27-28).

DEATH BRINGS LIFE

Jesus believed that he died on the cross to offer us new life, no longer bound by the habits of sin or the inevitability of our physical death. Jesus understands that without death, there can be no new life. Earlier, he had told his followers,

"The hour has come for the Son of Man to be glorified. Very truly, I tell you, unless a grain of wheat falls into the earth and dies, it remains just a single grain; but if it dies, it bears much fruit. Those who love their life lose it, and those who hate their life in this world will keep it for eternal life."

John 12:23-25

This is not simply a prediction about his life. It is instruction for ours. If you love your life, says Jesus, you will lose it. Death is part of the process. But who wants to die? We resist death at all costs. Our desire not to die is such a huge motivator that the levitical code of the Old Testament uses the threat of death to persuade people to avoid sin. There is a lot of putting to death in the Hebrew Bible:

- If you strike a person and they die, you will be put to death. (Exodus 21:12)
- If you kidnap a person, you will be put to death. (Exodus 21:16)
- If you profane the Sabbath, you will be put to death. (Exodus 31:14)
- If you offer your child as a sacrifice to the god Molech, you will be put to death. (Leviticus 20:2)
- If you swear against your mother or father, you will be put to death. (Leviticus 20:9)

The list just goes and on.

It seems that the prescription for sin was often death. The work of Jesus looked to put sin to death instead, so that we could all find life.

A few years ago, one of our daughters convinced me to build a raised-bed garden in our back yard. We pulled together some scrap lumber and nails, added the dirt and then bought plants and seeds. Seeds are amazing things. They are often the last thing a plant produces and are typically located at the end of a stem after the leaves have grown and the plant has matured. They spend their lifetime bathed in sunlight and enjoying the blue sky. For seeds to be useful, however, they have to fall from their stem, dry out a bit and then be buried in the ground. They have to die to their past life so that they can gain their new form and purpose. We buried the seeds in our garden and waited.

My daughter was skeptical, and she seemed to give up interest; until one day, she told me to come outside. We both admired the miracle of the shoots those tiny seeds sent up through the ground. In the days that followed, they grew and grew. From the unseen seeds in the ground below, new life had been raised. The days were getting hotter, and we knew the lettuce would not last much longer. We cut off the leaves. They were crisp and fresh. This daughter is not known for her love of salad, but she did not complain when she ate the lettuce those tiny seeds produced.

The pattern of death and resurrection is the chief framework we must embrace in order to emulate Christ in the love we live and offer others. That is not just true for Jesus. It is true for us as well. We must die if we are to live. That is why Jesus speaks of the other cross.

> [Jesus] said to them all, "If any want to become my followers, let them deny themselves and take up their cross daily and follow me. For those who want to save their life will lose it, and those who lose their life for my sake will save it. What does it profit them if they gain the whole world, but lose or forfeit themselves?"
>
> Luke 9:23-25

Jesus tells us that we will have to embrace the cross, the one that each of us is called to pick up as we follow Jesus on our journeys. We have to let those parts of our nature that are contrary to love die. Among others, we must let anger, contempt, unkindness, and our lack of grace, humility, forgiveness, and gentleness die. We die to our self-focused agendas, our bad habits, and our limiting preoccupations. We die to our obsession to be loved by everyone so that we can learn to offer love to anyone. We die to the craving to continuously have our way so that Christ can be Lord of our lives.

This does not mean that you will become less of yourself. You will not lose your unique personality, identity, or vibe. God delights in you being you. After all, it was God who made you. The basis of your identity, however, is the image of God, not the hurts that changed your personality years ago or the habits or hang-ups you have recently acquired. When we die to sin, we do not lose ourselves. We gain the capacity to take on the true beauty of the identity God designed for us. We must offer the inner space where the Holy Spirit can cultivate the secret garden of our soul. It requires attention, and a vision to what the landscape architect hoped would be expressed in the unique space of your life. Remove the briars and invasive species and slowly, the envisioned landscape is revealed. Beauty steadily gains its foothold and grows over time. Each season enables us to see its splendor in a fresh way, and with God's help, it becomes easier to maintain. Such a process is necessary if we are ever going to love like Jesus.

The journey to resurrection and new life necessarily includes death to the life that was "all about me." When our ego is assailed in such a way it will complain that we are being sacrificed, which is a circumstance few will embrace. This is why it is essential that we understand what is really at work in this transformation.

John Wooden coached UCLA to ten NCAA basketball championships. Seven of those happened consecutively. Wooden taught his players to live out "the pyramid of success," an image he used to describe character traits of a winning team. The third block in the pyramid he sketched out is called "team spirit." Under those words, Wooden originally wrote "the willingness to sacrifice personal interest or glory for the welfare of all."

He discovered however, that "team spirit" was the team's stumbling block, not a step to success. He observed that few would actually sacrifice when it mattered. Players did not pass the ball to others who had better position. They still took low percentage shots to increase their personal point totals. In the locker room, everyone thought they were willing to sacrifice for the welfare of the team. On the court, no one actually did. Wooden decided he had to be explicit and operationalize "team spirit." When he changed the description to read the *eagerness* "to sacrifice personal interest or glory for the welfare of all," everything changed.[5]

With this clear direction, the ball was passed, assists were made, rebounds were sought, and plays were followed, no matter who got the shot. Once his players became eager to sacrifice their personal interest for that of the team, they began to win game after game and take the championship.

Are you eager to allow your lesser self to die so that a new self can emerge and become more and more like Christ? This is how we gain the capacity to love consistently over time. It is important not to become transactional when we say that Jesus died for our sins. Jesus did not die to give us an entry ticket into heaven. He died so that we could transform. Christians who say they have salvation through Christ and who then speak and act like those in society who do not claim Jesus as Lord deceive themselves. When our lived values and our expectations for justice are no better than people who readily admit that they do not follow Jesus, our faith is empty and our discipleship is hollow.

This is why we must think beyond the event of forgiveness to its intended transformational outcome in our lives. To focus exclusively on our forgiveness as the outcome of Jesus' sacrifice is like taking your car for an oil change, coming for it later, and having this exchange with the technician:

"Did you change the oil?"

"Yes, we drained all the old oil out of it."

"Did you put the new oil in it?"

"Yes, we got all the old oil out and it was bad. It was a thick sludge. It is a good thing we got it out of there."

"Yes, but did you put new oil in it?"

"No. But we got all the old oil out."

You would be frustrated, because you wanted the vehicle to have new oil in its engine. Without new oil, you are going nowhere. Likewise, many of us who trust in Jesus for the forgiveness of our sins must also trust that Christ will pour his love into our lives so that we can take the journey he desires for us.

Without a doubt, the singular most important decision for those who want to love God, neighbor, and self consistently is not which bad habit to eliminate or which good work to begin. It is the decision to accept Jesus' love and forgiveness, and then make him Lord of your life. It is so much easier to enter the flow of loving others when Jesus leads and directs us.

Nothing changes a person as readily as a relationship with Jesus Christ where the values, priorities, and ways of Christ become our own. This type of relationship enables us to BE LOVE to others. To live this experience of Christian discipleship requires us to be mindful of the opportunities around us and how we are to be and act throughout our days.

Begin with Love

Expand the Circle

Lavish Love

Openhearted Love

Value the Vulnerable

Emulate Christ

We do well to remind ourselves continually that the ability to BE LOVE cannot be done on our own, but must be bound to our experience and understanding that before we do or become anything more, we are already BELOVED. We are children of God, on a journey with Jesus, growing in the likeness of our Creator as we love with a reckless abandon, and a dedication to see the Great Commandment become the defining reality of our lives.

EPILOGUE

All journeys come to an end. Climbers who scale the summit of the mountain and enjoy the breathtaking vista will finally follow the trail to the parking lot. The boy who rides his bike in a nearby park, skips rocks with his friends on the pond, and shoots basketball on the court nearby eventually goes home for dinner. The newlyweds who peer over the top of the Eiffel Tower to see Paris at night, absorb the color and style of the Impressionists at the Musée d'Orsay, and stroll and dawdle on the Champs-Élysées eventually return to their one-bedroom apartment and office cubicles. Families who stand on the edge of the Grand Canyon, enjoy a four-wheel drive tour through the red rock of Sedona, and hike through the hillsides of Flagstaff arrive home to grass that needs to be mowed, a dog that begs to be walked, and mail piled on the kitchen counter. All good things must come to an end. But as they say, when one journey ends, another begins.

The male disciples heard Jesus predict his resurrection. Yet, when the women came to tell them that they had seen Jesus, and even spoken to him in the garden outside his tomb, they did not accept the news as true. It wasn't until they saw Jesus with their own eyes, heard the voice of the resurrected Lord, and connected the memory of his words with the reality of their experience that they believed such a thing was possible.

Jesus appeared to them several times. He probably needed to, in order to convince each one that resurrection was possible. I can see why the resurrection is so difficult for people to believe who don't know Jesus. The faith of those who did not enjoy Jesus' presence, who did not hear his voice or see his wounded hands, requires us to intellectually ascend to the conviction that he was God incarnate. The disciples saw in order to believe. We must believe in order to see. This required step of faith may be why Jesus told his first followers, "Because you have seen me, you have believed; blessed are those who have not seen and yet have believed" (John 20:29 NIV).

Either way, the reality of Jesus' resurrection is indispensable for our ability to love others. Jesus had to find new life in order to give us the hope that it could happen for us as well. Usually when Christians speak of the Resurrection, it is in the context of life after death. Jesus did talk about our place in heaven and the nature of eternal life. But he spent far more time talking about the reality of new life here and now.

Jesus understood that if his followers were going to live out the Great Commandment to love God, neighbor, and self, they would have to rise up out of the quagmire of thoughts and habits formed without his influence and reinforced by the society in which they lived. They would have to be resurrected to a new life as those who both understood the teaching of Christ and had the desire and willingness to be empowered daily by the Holy Spirit to live it out. The disciples understood that if Christ was resurrected from the dead, the lessons of their journey would not be the cherished memory of a uniquely blessed portion of their life. The new life he offered could be their own. Jesus' way of life, his ability to be love to others and help people realize that they were beloved of God, could be the way they lived as well.

I have friends who loved to spend time at the beach. As a couple they planned getaways to slow down, take a swim, and walk together on the sand. They enjoyed summer vacations with their family at the ocean. They collected shells, rode the waves, built spacious sand castles, and flew kites among the seagulls who flew past on warm summer evenings. When the time came for retirement, they thought about all of those great vacations and realized that environment was the one they preferred. Rather than visit, they decided to move there. Now they watch the sunrise on the water any day of the year. They protect turtles who lay their eggs in the sand. They walk on the beach anytime they want. While other people enjoy the ocean when they visit for a few days or a week, our friends have made it their home.

Being made new in Christ means the difference between being a person who loves the Lord with all his or her heart, soul, and strength, and one who worships God when it's convenient, loves others on occasion, or in a well-intended chain of events that includes links regretfully broken by periods of insecurity and self-centeredness. It is the person who seeks the will of God daily in contrast to the one who indulges the blissfully ignorant mind that has embraced the belief that the news of human hunger, injustice, or the suffering of the oppressed is simply too bad to be true. It is the difference between the person whose heart breaks and whose hands work to relieve the suffering of others, and the one who sometimes takes a quick jaunt of compassion, but mostly lives insulated from the world soaking in the warm spa waters of self-absorption.

Jesus did not simply show them a resurrection, he called his disciples to live a resurrected life. He met with them one last time before he ascended into heaven. Some hoped he would complete the journey in a dramatic flourish. They asked him, "Lord, is this the time when you will restore the kingdom to Israel?" (Acts 1:6).

I picture Jesus' smile as he hears the question. They still want him to do the heavy lifting. They hope to take in the next wonder. Jesus has no intention of such an outcome. He wants them to have a new life. He wants them to help usher in the kingdom of God as it breaks into the world. He wants them to be miracle workers, not miracle watchers. Jesus is telling them to leave what is familiar and take up residence in a new way of life. He replies,

> "It is not for you to know the times or periods that the Father has set by his own authority. But you will receive power when the Holy Spirit has come upon you; and you will be my witnesses in Jerusalem, in all Judea and Samaria, and to the ends of the earth."
>
> Acts 1:7-8

Many call this series of locations—Jerusalem, Judea, Samaria—the "ever-widening circle." Jerusalem was the capital of their religion and culture. The nexus of Judaism was the Temple, the focal point of the city and the place to which the people of Israel made an annual pilgrimage from distant lands where they lived. It was called the "holy city" because its citizens believed that God dwelt there. Jerusalem was full of the familiar. The food was easy to eat, the language was effortless for the disciples to understand, the patterns of daily life were all well-known there. Judea was the surrounding countryside. It too was familiar. It included the Sea of Galilee and its surrounding villages, from which many of them had come.

Samaria was a place they had been taught to avoid and included a people they had been taught to discount as both spiritually unclean and culturally uncouth. It is not a place you go to. It is a place you make yourself go to. You know that if you choose to go there, you will have to learn a lot about the Samaritans. And you will have to unlearn a lot about the Samaritans that others taught you that is simply not consistent with what you observe when you finally get to know them. Samaria is a place that will make you tired because of all the thinking and considering, the learning and unlearning that is required if you are going to be love in that space.

No phrase was more unfamiliar than "the ends of the earth." To a group of people who had never traveled more than a few hundred miles in one direction in their entire lifetime, "the ends of the earth" may have been a bit daunting. Here Jesus called them to spread Christianity throughout the Roman Empire, into Africa, and across the east to what we now call India and beyond. The minds of the first disciples could not conceive of the grand vision Jesus offered in these five words. Most of the earth was unknown to them. The tribes, cultures, and civilizations that Jesus' message of love would eventually reach and transform were beyond their comprehension. The part they did understand, however, was remarkable. Just the thought that some of them might travel to Rome, the capital of the Empire, to tell others about Christ, probably exceeded the limits of their imagination.

It was good that Jesus began his description of their mission with the encouragement that they would be empowered by the Holy Spirit. I doubt any of them embraced Jesus' direction with great confidence that he had the right people for the tasks ahead. However, it was probably not lost on them that the journey that Jesus now drew to a close had already taken them everywhere he now told them to go. They had seen Jesus, in the familiarity of Jerusalem, challenging a set of expectations and even centuries-old teachings of the other rabbis and teachers of the law in surprising ways. They had walked all over Judea, seen the needs of people who were sick and the crowds that longed for wise teaching. They had spent a few nights in Samaria, met people, learned names, and enjoyed the hospitality of those who lived there. They had seen Jesus interact with Roman soldiers, stand before Pontius Pilate, and use the power of the Resurrection to overcome the dominance and oppression of the Empire.

There was no place Jesus commanded them to go that they had not, in some way, already been. Before he sent them out into this ever-widening circle, he had widened their circles and expanded their relational world to include people they could never imagine knowing, much less sitting with at a dinner table. The journey with Jesus, this three-year immersion in the kingdom of God, was now to become their home. Where one journey ends, a new one begins. They could not move back to their past homes, buy back their fishing boats, or regain a tax collection franchise. Luke begins his account of the Acts of the Apostles here, understanding that the disciples were given a great commission to fulfill the Great Commandment. This was to be their continued way of life.

We must see this clearly, or we will miss the point of our life in Christ. Christ's followers today receive the same calling and commission. If we miss this, it will have consequences. Rather than be witnesses to Christ in the way we love God, others, and ourselves, we will begin to think that Jesus came to make us nicer or a little more thoughtful, the kind of people who remember birthdays and select more personal Christmas gifts. Rather than tell others about God's grace or offer mercy, we will believe that living a Christian life is about feeling forgiven of our sins. Rather than telling others about the habit-changing, bondage-breaking, turnaround-making power Jesus can have in our lives, we will cultivate a relationship with Christ that is so personal that we never share it with anyone else. Rather than speaking out and working for justice with those who hold position and power in our community and society, we will spend our time telling the already convinced how much better the world would be if it were not exactly as it is. Rather than offering acts of solace to those who grieve, comfort to the sick, or kindness of conversation with prisoners or returning citizens, we will simply offer thanks that we are not in such predicaments ourselves.

Jesus takes us on a journey so that he can deploy us on a mission. He offers his love to us so that we will share it with the world. He does this because he loves us. The first disciples knew they were beloved, not only because of what Jesus did for them, but because Jesus believed in them when he called them to go to Jerusalem, Judea, Samaria, and the ends of the earth. He knew what they could do for him. Jesus believed in them more than they believed in themselves. He saw more potential in them than they ever thought possible in their lives. He forgave them for what they were not, just as he celebrated all that they were. All of this is what is at the heart of being beloved by another. When we are beloved, we gain the confidence another has in us and make it our own. That confidence transforms how we think of ourselves. It guides the journey that, in the end, leads to who we become. Such love, once extended, is what stirs up a new sense of possibility in our lives.

This is the love God has for you, and the belief God holds in you. We must have faith that God believes in us, in our ability to love our neighbor, to treat ourselves properly in this life, and to worship the Lord with our heart, mind, soul, and strength.

Now the short excursion that is this book comes to an end. But I hope that for you, it will be the beginning of a renewed journey of discipleship with Jesus, a renewed quest for the ongoing experience of love. I am sure that the One who created you believes in your ability to actually live this commandment as your way of life.

ACKNOWLEDGMENTS

Nothing is done without the support and kindness of people around you. I am especially grateful for the willingness of my wife, Karen, to read the manuscript and offer her suggestions. Her understanding of the teaching of Christ, the insights of the Bible, and the joy of loving others is a well of insight.

My assistant, Pam Borland, kindly looked at these pages and offered helpful corrections to my writing. She routinely helps me be more competent than I would be on my own. The pastoral staff at Floris UMC, along with Mark Rader, allowed me the time to put this together in an already busy season. They are true colleagues in ministry and I am grateful for their support.

The encouragement of leaders at Floris to undertake this project is another reason that I have enjoyed such a long relationship with the church. Thanks to Donna Wolfersberger for the tour of Oatlands and for first telling me the story of Robert Carter III.

This book is full of people whose lives have touched and influenced my own. I am grateful to you all. Charlie Kendall and Moonbounce Media created the videos for this series. Their creativity and commitment to quality are always expressed in their work. Finally, thanks to Susan Salley and Maria Mayo at Abingdon, along with those who added value to this project whose names I do not know. Your encouragement to write, understanding of my schedule, and your work to improve what I write, are both prized and appreciated.

NOTES

Chapter 1, Begin with Love

1. C. S. Lewis, *Mere Christianity* (Macmillan, 1943; reprint Simon & Schuster, 1996), 116.
2. M. Lejars, A. Margaillan, and C. Bressy, "Fouling Release Coatings: A Nontoxic Alternative to Biocidal Antifouling Coatings" (Chemical Reviews, vol. 112, no. 8, May 2012), 4347–4390. Retrieved from https://pubs.acs.org/doi/10.1021/cr200350v. Accessed October 15, 2018.
3. Barbara Brown Taylor, *An Altar in the World: A Geography of Faith* (New York: Harper-Collins, 2009), 93.

Chapter 2, Expand the Circle

1. Dorothy Day, *All the Way to Heaven: The Selected Letters of Dorothy Day* (New York: Image Books, 2010), 326.
2. *How the Grinch Stole Christmas!* Video, directed by Chuck Jones (Los Angeles: Warner Bros., 1966).
3. Dr. Seuss [pseud.], *How the Grinch Stole Christmas!* (New York: Random House, 1957; reprint Random House, 1985).
4. *How the Grinch Stole Christmas!* Video, directed by Chuck Jones.
5. Maria Konnikova, "The Limits of Friendship" (*The New Yorker*, October 7, 2014). Retrieved November 20, 2018, from https://www.newyorker.com/science/maria-konnikova/social-media-affect-math-dunbar-number-friendships. Accessed January 3, 2019.

6. TEDx Talk, March 21, 2012. *Robin Dunbar: Can the internet buy you more friends?* [Video file]. Retrieved November 20, 2018, from https://www.youtube.com/watch?v=07IpED729k8.

Chapter 3, Lavish Love

1. Martin Buber, *On Judaism: An Introduction to the Essence of Judaism by One of the Most Important Religious Thinkers of the Twentieth Century* (New York: Schocken Books, 1996), 212.
2. Eli Rosenberg, "'I'm Dr. Cohen': The powerful humanity of the Jewish hospital staff that treated Robert Bowers" (*The Washington Post*, October 30, 2018). Retrieved from https://www.washingtonpost.com/health/2018/10/30/im-dr-cohen-powerful-humanity-jewish-hospital-staff-that-treated-robert-bowers/?utm_term=.bf96f13a7a26. Accessed December 28, 2018.
3. Harriet McLeod, Alana Wise, and Luciana Lopez, "Families of South Carolina church massacre victims offer forgiveness" (Reuters, June 18, 2015). Retrieved from https://www.reuters.com/article/us-usa-shooting-south-carolina/families-of-south-carolina-church-massacre-victims-offer-forgiveness-idUSKBN0OY06A20150619. Accessed December 28, 2018.
4. Eddie Pipkin, "Bonsai Thinking," Excellence in Ministry Coaching, 2016. Retrieved from https://emc3coaching.com/bonsai-thinking/?inf_contact_key=eba832ce373ea2de42bc2049c3ed8e40062ee192e524820c00bc068496661637. Accessed December 1, 2018.
5. Wesley Study Bible. "Wesleyan Core Term: 'Gratitude and Benevolence'" (Nashville: Abingdon Press, 2009), 1260.
6. Martin Buber, *I and Thou* (New York: Charles Scribner's Sons, 1937; reprint Continuum International Publishing Group, 2004).

Chapter 4, Openhearted Love

1. Mark Twain, *The Innocents Abroad* (CreateSpace Independent Publishing Platform, 2017), 343.
2. Frederick Douglass, 1818–1895. *Narrative of the Life of Frederick Douglass, an American Slave* (Tribeca Books, 2010), 105–106.
3. Mariah Burton Nelson, "The Word Was 'Agitate'" (*The Washington Post*, November 4, 2018). Retrieved from https://www.washingtonpost.com/archive/lifestyle/1988/11/04/the-word-was-agitate/145738e8-5b66-4152

-9bba-270956c4d4fd/?utm_term=.8e5a34239834. Accessed December 1, 2018.

4. Kenneth Bailey, *Jesus Through Middle Eastern Eyes* (Downers Grove, IL: InterVarsity Press, 2008), 189–194.

5. Ibid.

6. "Tragedy in Charlottesville: The Unite the Right rally" (*USA Today*, July 23, 2018). Retrieved from https://www.usatoday.com/videos/news/politics /2018/07/23/tragedy-charlottesville-unite-right-rally/817968002/. Accessed November 1, 2018.

7. Richard K. MacMaster, "Liberty or Property? The Methodists Petition for Emancipation in Virginia, 1785" (The United Methodist General Commission on Archives and History, October 1, 1971), 44–45. Retrieved from http://archives.gcah.org/handle/10516/1669?show=full. Accessed November 30, 2018.

8. Brendan Wolfe, "Robert Carter III's Deed of Gift" (Encyclopedia Virginia, May 5, 2017). Retrieved from https://www.encyclopediavirginia.org /Deed_of_Gift_Robert_Carter_III_s#start_entry. Accessed November 30, 2018.

9. "Loving V. Virginia," History.com editors, August 21, 2018. Retrieved from https://www.history.com/topics/civil-rights-movement/loving-v-virginia. Accessed November 30, 2018.

10. Rex Springston, "Happy slaves? The peculiar story of three Virginia school textbooks" (*Richmond Times-Dispatch*, April 14, 2018). Retrieved from https://www.richmond.com/discover-richmond/happy-slaves-the-peculiar -story-of-three-virginia-school-textbooks/article_47e79d49-eac8-575d -ac9d-1c6fce52328f.html. Accessed November 30, 2018.

Chapter 5, Value the Vulnerable

1. Booker T. Washington, *Up From Slavery: An Autobiography*, Volume 3 (New York: Doubleday, Page & Co., 1901), 66.

2. Alexandra Petri, "Bad job, Self" (*The Washington Post*, March 27, 2014). Retrieved from https://www.washingtonpost.com/blogs/compost/wp /2014/03/27/bad-job-self/?utm_term=.b21130b7fc29. Accessed December 2, 2018.

3. Ibid.

Chapter 6, Emulate Christ

1. Fred Rogers, *You Are Special: Words of Wisdom for All Ages from a Beloved Neighbor* (New York: Viking, 1994), 17.
2. "Royals end Alcides Escobar's consecutive games streak at 421" (ESPN News Services, July 8, 2018). Retrieved from http://www.espn.com/mlb /story/_/id/24040662/alcides-escobar-games-played-streak-end-421. Accessed October 1, 2018.
3. Allison Klein, "Lost wallet returned, with something extra inside" (*The Washington Post*, November 27, 2018). Retrieved from https://www .washingtonpost.com/lifestyle/2018/11/27/lost-wallet-returned-with -something-extra-inside/?noredirect=on&utm_term=.61d9b3263c9c& wpisrc=nl_inspired&wpmm=1. Accessed October 1, 2018.
4. Edited by George Lyons, "A Plain Account of Christian Perfection" (The Wesley Center for Applied Theology at Northwest Nazarene University). Retrieved from http://wesley.nnu.edu/john-wesley/a-plain-account-of -christian-perfection/. Accessed December 28, 2018.
5. John Wooden with Steve Jamison, *Wooden: A Lifetime of Observations and Reflections On and Off the Court* (Chicago: Contemporary Books, 1997), 188–189.